"Reading Rivadeneira's *Broke* brings the Beatitudes to life. With in-your-face honesty riddled with mirthful profundity, she takes her reader around blind corners smack into the glory and goodness of God. Rivadeneira reminds us that the abundant life is quite a ride, and that our ticket has been paid in full. All we have to pay is our attention."

Carolyn Weber, author of *Holy Is the Day* and *Surprised by Oxford*

"Caryn Rivadeneira may be broke, but she's also brave. For some reason, it takes guts to admit you're in real financial trouble, and she shares her story boldly and without shame. So many others will relate to her. But the real beauty is that this is not essentially a story of losing money. It's about gaining a new sense for God's redemptive presence in her disappointment, hardship, fear and frustration. Her story may help you recognize him in your places of pain too."

Amy Simpson, author of *Troubled Minds* and editor of Christianity Today's GiftedForLeadership.com

"If you like your Jesus sugary sweet, don't read *Broke*. If you don't think irreverent humor is next to godliness, don't read *Broke*. If you hope that being broken by God involves superficial tinkering, not soul-deep wrenching, don't read *Broke*. If you don't want a faith strong enough to wrestle with agonizing questions and hard stories, don't read *Broke*. But if you like gritty and funny, honest and faithful, go for *Broke*."

Karen Swallow Prior, author of *Booked: Literature in the Soul of Me*

"Only Caryn Rivadeneira could weave a tale of financial desperation into a page-turner. I didn't want to put it down at night. You will discover life and light in these beautifully written pages."

Margot Starbuck, author of *Small Things with Great Love*

"I loved this book! A great read for those of us who need reminding that God doesn't ever leave us out to dry. God is present in all of life, and Caryn brings that peace to light in this great read."

Rev. Tracey Bianchi, pastor, Christ Church of Oak Brook

Caryn Rivadeneira

BR⬤KE

What Financial Desperation
Revealed About God's Abundance

IVP Books

An imprint of InterVarsity Press
Downers Grove, Illinois

InterVarsity Press
P.O. Box 1400, Downers Grove, IL 60515-1426
World Wide Web: www.ivpress.com
Email: email@ivpress.com

InterVarsity Press® is the book-publishing division of InterVarsity Christian Fellowship/USA®, a
movement of students and faculty active on campus at hundreds of universities, colleges and schools of
nursing in the United States of America, and a member movement of the International Fellowship of
Evangelical Students. For information about local and regional activities, write Public Relations Dept.,
InterVarsity Christian Fellowship/USA, 6400 Schroeder Rd., P.O. Box 7895, Madison, WI 53707-7895,
or visit the IVCF website at www.intervarsity.org.

All Scripture quotations, unless otherwise indicated, are taken from the Holy Bible, Today's New
International Version™ Copyright © 2001 by International Bible Society. All rights reserved.

While all stories in this book are true, some names and identifying information in this book have been
changed to protect the privacy of the individuals involved.

Cover design: Cindy Kiple
Interior design: Beth Hagenberg
Images: Walker and Walker/Getty Images

ISBN 978-0-8308-4311-4 (print)
ISBN 978-0-8308-8402-5 (digital)

Printed in the United States of America ∞

Library of Congress Cataloging-in-Publication Data
A catalog record for this book is available from the Library of Congress.

P	17	16	15	14	13	12	11	10	9	8	7	6	5	4	3	2	1
Y	28	27	26	25	24	23	22	21	20	19	18	17	16	15	14

To Rafi

Contents

Going for Broke

Listen to your life.
See it for the fathomless mystery it is.
In the boredom and pain of it, no less than in the
excitement and gladness: touch, taste, smell your way
to the holy and hidden heart of it, because in the
last analysis all moments are key moments,
and life itself is grace.

Frederick Buechner,
Now and Then: A Memoir of Vocation

Once upon a time—well, the first full day my husband and I were married, actually—we met a man. He had wheeled our luggage up from the glorious lobby of the Ritz-Carlton hotel, over the lush rugs, past the glittering china cabinets, around the circular foyer tables adorned with huge sprays of flowers, to our equally glorious room, all yellow and fresh and cozy, on the seventh floor. Somewhere in the elevator, while we adjusted ourselves around the brass luggage cart, and he apologized for any inconvenience, and after having discussed our newlywed-ed status and post-wedding exhaustion and exhilaration, the bellhop asked us what we did.

My husband went first. "I manage money for individuals," Rafi said, as he always did.

"You work for yourself?" the bellhop asked.

"Yes," Rafi said. "My partner and I started the firm two years ago."

"Going well?" the man asked.

"Better every day."

"I did that too, once," the bellhop said. And then the story began: our bellhop had managed hedge funds, but he had ended up losing at a "game" all others around him seemed to win.

While I was restless to get rid of the man, eager to get on with our honeymoon, finding his story unnecessarily depressing for a couple just starting our life, my husband remained engrossed. He wanted to hear what had gone wrong, and how he had ended up moving from managing money on Wall Street to carting luggage on a Florida beach.

"Oh, lots of things went wrong," the bellhop said as he pushed open the door to our room. "And after not being able to 'right' the wrongs, I realized it was okay. More than anything, I just didn't want that life anymore. All that chasing. All that greed." And then, with a wave of his arm across our room toward the balcony and the sun that glimmered on the Gulf of Mexico beyond it, he added, "And somehow, I found you can lose everything and gain something better."

My husband nodded, thanked him and handed him a tip. I rolled my eyes as I closed the door behind him. With that I had hoped this man was out of our lives and our marriage, and that his story would get woven so deep into the fabric of our lives together that it'd disappear, or only reappear in funny little honeymoon stories that began with "Remember that weird guy . . ."

But instead, that bellhop remained a reoccurring character in our marriage. Not in the flesh, of course, but as one whom my husband would refer back to through the years. First, as my husband's business soared and succeeded, as he achieved every financial and business goal he sought, the bellhop would come up every now and again with a question, "What could he have gotten tired of? Wonder what went wrong?"

And then, later, when my husband started realizing he too was getting tired of the chase and worn down from the greed, the bellhop would emerge again—a new understanding this time.

But it wasn't until the day I looked at the numbers—at the stat that told me how close my family's income level had come to the poverty line that year, and at the ever-increasing weight of medical debt that we labored and moaned and groaned to pay down—that I realized the bellhop and his words and his little motioning hand weren't some oddity.

I realized my husband had been as wise to listen to his words as I had been foolish to toss them away. Because that bellhop was a prophet, speaking the truth of our future right as it began.

Had I listened, had I heeded, we might have sidestepped all this. But I didn't. Or maybe, at least, had I grasped it much earlier, maybe we could have dealt with it in a much less painful way. But I just couldn't. Who would've imagined?

Anyone who knew us would've agreed: *broke* was not in the cards for us. Not, that is, after we waded through the newlywed, one-starting-a-new-business, the-other-working-in-entry-level publishing phase. Of course, *then* it was all about broke. As it should be. But still. We were the kind of couple who married with such material promise. Broke should never have happened. Not to the couple who danced their first wedded dance in one of the swankiest ballrooms in Chicago, who opened wedding gifts of Tiffany silver and china place settings. Couples destined for broke don't get gifts like that. Nor do they rent tiny apartments for years until a proper down payment could be had. Nor do they purchase a home at far below what banks approve them for and furnish it with family-member castoffs. I'm pretty sure couples destined for broke do not live below their means for years and plunk big chunks of their income into retirement and regular savings accounts. Couples destined for broke do not give faithfully—or, pretty faithfully—to church and various charities. Because God blesses that sort of thing. Financially.

And yet.

Broke was not in the cards for me. Not the girl with the good head on her shoulders and the bright brain within it. Not the one with the sort of confidence that had stunned her shyness into submission as she stepped into the world like no monsters ever lurked in it. Girls with common sense, bravado, a healthy sense of humor and a solid faith do not grow up to break. Especially not girls who grow into women who write and take their Common-Sense, Ha-Ha, God-Is-Good show on the road. Girls— then women—like us stay strong through it all. A little (or big) financial setback doesn't break us. Or our connection to God.

And yet.

And yet, when my husband and I asked God if we were really living as we should be, as he would want, when we asked him to put us on the path he'd have us, God let us go broke. Dead broke. We got caught in a horrible swirl of depressed housing markets, of sagging businesses, of long periods of under-employment and then unemployment, of debt from uncovered medical expenses. All of this hit at once, leaving us wondering where on earth we'd land, dependent on the kindness of family and friends to even attempt to make ends meet.

And yet, when I asked God to let me find him (*really* find him) and to know him (*really* know him) and to see him and smell him and taste him and sense his presence and his wondrousness all over the darned place like I had as a kid, he broke me. Clean open. Snapped and shattered.

And yet.

We survived. I kept breathing. I kept stepping. And somewhere in the cracks, along the ragged edges of my marriage, in the desperate gasps of sudden poverty and all the questions that came with it, there was God. Big and glittering, soft and warm, smiling and beckoning. Somehow in the shimmers of all that, I began to taste and see, and feel and know, and hear and smell that God is good, and he was there in the broke bits. That he was using our time near the poverty line, treading in debt, to draw me near, to make me over, to answer a prayer bigger than my material needs. In this season of spiritual and financial brokenness, in this time of longing to know what God was up to and to experience his goodness and presence, God worked me over by showing me where and how I could find him. Which is all over the place. In every last thing. He satisfied my *wonderlust*— my unquenchable desire to feel his presence and to experience his glory. And I found him. And I found him good.

Heard

One Sunday afternoon, my son sidled up alongside me as I plunked away at my laptop, and he slid a homemade church bulletin across the keyboard (my kids know how to get their mom's attention). He and his younger brother and sister had been busy moving sofas, crafting bulletins and practicing songs—all for the church service they planned in the living room. Apparently, however, not one of them felt like preaching, and they needed a sermon. Stat.

"Mom," my son said, "can you preach on faithfulness today? And be ready in ten minutes?"

"Sure," I said. "I can talk about being faithful, no sweat."

He rolled his eyes. "Not about *being* faithful. Talk about *God's* faithfulness. Can you do *that?*"

"You bet," I lied.

Truth was, my son caught me just two hours after an actual church service in which I had fought back tears of frustration, and in which I lacked the energy to even pretend to pray or sing. I was in no mood to be worship-y with God that morning. Nor was I in any mood to offers nice words on God's faithfulness that afternoon.

The trouble was that that day was one of *those* days. A sermon on giving had stirred up old wounds and rote prayers. I didn't need to be reminded that faithful giving was a spiritual discipline. I knew that. But while *I* didn't need reminding, I thought perhaps *God* did. After all, it'd been his trinitarian counterpart who'd bestowed "giving" on me as a spiritual gift. And you'd think folks gifted in such a way would also be given the materials with which to give.

So I'd been grumbling at God about that. Again. Reminding him about how dire our situation was becoming. About how much more work either I needed or my husband needed if we were to keep paying the mortgage or to pay these bills. I reminded God about that third child he'd surprised us with, and how we trusted that he would help us cover yet another hospital birth without maternity insurance—and yet how the debt from that was mounting even as our income was sinking. And I prayed again that my husband find a different job, if that was God's will. Or that his business would find its feet again, if that were. I reminded God that I had a couple of books in print—he could send a few hundred thousand folks out to buy copies. How hard would that be for God? Not hard at all. And how good would that be for us? So good.

But I had already prayed these prayers more times than I could count—to no avail. We'd gotten no new jobs, no clear guidance, no path out of debt, no financial rescue, no hundreds of thousands of book buyers. *Not yet*, I tried to think. But more and more, *not ever* replaced it.

That afternoon that my son came to me, I'd asked what I thought would be my last time—that God would come through, that he would solve our financial crunch, help us climb our way out of debt, help us restore the savings that we had now burned through. That he do this so that—so that!—we could get back to giving. And so that our marriage could get out from under so much stress. So that our family could once again have moments of happiness, of frivolity even.

But I doubted he would. Where once in my life God had been so present and good and near, and where once he whispered into my life and revealed himself all around, now I wondered where he was. Or *if* he was.

So now I was supposed to talk about God's faithfulness—in front of my kids? *That* was going to be a problem.

"Mom, you ready?" my son yelled from the living room.

As I straightened my legs, scooting my chair across the wood floor, I yelled back, "Be right there," and turned my face up.

All right, God, I prayed. One last time. One new prayer. *Can you at least help me out here? Can you help me tell these guys about your faithfulness and that you hear and that sometimes, with some people, you've actually responded to prayers? Can you make it so I don't have to lie?*

And then, after all that time of me left feeling high and dry, unheard and alone, wandering a wilderness with my shoulders shrugged and my hands up, of pouring out my heart for some big need and rough situations, desperate for a word, a sighting, a whiff, an anything from God, God said, *Okay,* and he brought me right back to the first time I'd known him to be faithful.

Although seven was among my all-time favorite ages, and among the most formative ages of my life (it was the age I remember first wanting to follow Jesus, as well as when I knew I wanted to be a writer), the year also plagued me with headaches.

Several days a week, I'd wake up with a stiff neck and a throbbing head, and I'd beg to stay home from school. Some days I was allowed to; others, the baby aspirin kicked in and I was off. Happily.

But the headaches were persistent enough and baffled my pediatrician and then neurologist enough that my newly born-again Christian parents listened to the elders in our charismatic Lutheran church, who thought they should anoint me with oil and lay hands on my head for healing.

Of course, the laying on of hands and anointing with oil comes straight out of Scripture. Were one of my kids as stricken as I was during that time, I'd consider the same thing. However, when I was seven, and not yet too keen on this whole church-and-Holy-Spirit business that my parents had so wildly come to embrace, this little idea of strangers touching my head and dripping olive oil on my blond Dorothy Hamill didn't go over well with me. Not at all.

But, alas, my protests did nothing (in my parents' defense, they wanted me better!), and one Sunday after church, I sat down on the steps that led up to the altar, encircled by my parents and a couple of elders. Each laid their hands on my head. They all prayed fervently and faithfully that God would heal me, that he would remove the "demons" (this is the word that I remember, though my mother categorically denies this) that caused the headaches, and that I would know God's healing power and mercy through this experience. The elders prayed loudly and dramatically. One hand on my head. Another lifted to heaven. Men of the church and all.

In the meantime, my little body tensed. My face scrunched. My fingers picked at the nails on the other hand. I may have lost the battle with my parents, but I saw the war as far from over. I was taking this up with God.

As the "O yes, Lords" rang around me, I offered my own little prayer: *God, I don't want this to work. Don't listen to them.*

Please hear me. I'd rather have headaches than this.

The whole prayer lasted probably less than two minutes. Then we got up, small-talked some and left. My family stopped at Grandma Sally's Pancake House for brunch on the way home. In many ways, it was a usual Sunday. But that day changed me. That day launched my lifelong, often-embattled faith journey.

In fact, the next morning, I woke up a new person. Born again. Healed. Because as I rubbed my tight, aching neck and pressed my fingers against my throbbing temples, desperate to relieve yet another headache, I knew: God heard my prayers. Above the show and the oil and the raised-high, holy hands, I knew that God heard *me*, the little one, cowering in the middle.

I knew he heard me. And that God was good. And my life would never be the same.

Now plenty of people out there would be willing to consider my headache the next day to be pure coincidence. Or self-induced, maybe. After all, a person can stress herself into having a headache. And truth be told, over the course of that year, my persistent headaches did go away. Since that time of my life, I rarely get headaches of that caliber or frequency. God actually did answer those elders' prayers. And I'm glad he did.

But much more powerful than being healed of any headache was waking up with a killer one the next day. And realizing that God heard *me*. It kicked off a lifelong journey of following a God who I understood wanted a relationship with me, listening to shy little me above the cries of older and wiser and churchier sorts.

I chose to believe this then. And—even as I replay this time in my life from the vantage point of me thirty-plus years older,

wiser and more "spiritual"—I choose to believe it still now. This
is *not* to say I've never stopped believing it. I'd love to say that
once I chose to believe that God was eager to speak to me, to
show his goodness to me—through a headache, through my
senses, through pain, through experience—that I never forgot
this. But the truth is, I often forgot it. Or, more precisely: I chose
to ignore it. To *not* believe it. That's where the trouble began.

When I allowed my senses to dull to God's faithfulness, I
dulled to God completely. When I stopped paying attention to
all the ways that God was good, when I stopped noticing that
God *was* good, all the time, I stopped believing it. When I ignored God and the ways his fingers of love and mercy ran over
every bit of my life, I felt ignored by God. I blamed him for his
absence, his infidelity. Turns out, I was the unfaithful one.

Hagar's story is one of my new favorites. I'm overwhelmed with
guilt and sadness that I've spent a lifetime glossing over her story
in favor of the "bigger names" she's mixed in with—namely, her
master Abram and her cruel mistress, Sarai. As I've discovered,
however, Hagar is definitely not a woman you want to lose
sight of. God sure didn't. And that's what makes her otherwise-
horrifying story so beautiful.

The horrifying part is this: when Sarai couldn't bear children
for Abram, she offered up her personal slave, Hagar, to sleep
with him. Think about this. Imagine your boss can't have a baby
and decides that you should sleep with her husband. And that
you don't have a choice.

Genesis 16:3 says, "So . . . Sarai his wife took her Egyptian
servant Hagar and gave her to her husband to be his wife." *Took*

and *gave* make this sound almost generous, but we're talking rape. Violence. Forced "breeding." No doubt about this here. This is awful stuff from Father Abraham and Mother Sarah. And it doesn't get better.

When Hagar conceives, she begins to "despise her mistress" (Genesis 16:4). No wonder she does! It's the only tiny power play an otherwise powerless woman can use.

But of course, Sarai, powerless in her own right as a barren woman, won't stand for this from her slave. So she goes to Abram who tells her to deal with Hagar as she sees fit (Genesis 16:6). Considering what she's already done to her, I can hardly imagine the horror of what ensued, but what we do know is that it was bad enough for a pregnant, powerless, penniless woman to run away from the only source of "protection" she otherwise had.

Here's the scene, straight from Genesis 16:4-16:

> He slept with Hagar, and she conceived.
>
> When she knew she was pregnant, she began to despise her mistress. Then Sarai said to Abram, "You are responsible for the wrong I am suffering. I put my servant in your arms, and now that she knows she is pregnant, she despises me. May the LORD judge between you and me."
>
> "Your servant is in your hands," Abram said. "Do with her whatever you think best." Then Sarai mistreated Hagar, so she fled from her.
>
> The angel of the LORD found Hagar near a spring in the desert; it was the spring that is beside the road to Shur. And he said, "Hagar, servant of Sarai, where have you come from, and where are you going?"
>
> "I'm running away from my mistress Sarai," she answered.
>
> Then the angel of the LORD told her, "Go back to your mistress and submit to her." The angel added, "I will

increase your descendants so much that they will be too
numerous to count."

The angel of the LORD also said to her:

> "You are now pregnant
> and you will give birth to a son.
> You shall name him Ishmael,
> for the LORD has heard of your misery.
> He will be a wild donkey of a man;
> his hand will be against everyone
> and everyone's hand against him,
> and he will live in hostility
> toward all his brothers."

She gave this name to the LORD who spoke to her: "You
are the God who sees me," for she said, "I have now seen
the One who sees me." That is why the well was called Beer
Lahai Roi; it is still there, between Kadesh and Bered.

So Hagar bore Abram a son, and Abram gave the name
Ishmael to the son she had borne. Abram was eighty-six
years old when Hagar bore him Ishmael.

Out of this scene, we learn three of the most important (is this
too audacious to say?) things we can know about God: (1) that
he hears us (Ishmael); (2) that he sees us (*El Roi*); and (3) that
the God of Abraham, the God of us, didn't create us and move
on. He didn't change the channel and turn his attention to more
interesting creatures elsewhere in this universe. He sees us and
he hears us and—get this—he stops in to chat with us.

Sarai (and Abram) might not have thought much of Hagar,
but God did. *God did!* Of all the things God had going on at that
moment in history, he popped over to hang with Hagar. To let
her know he saw and heard her.

He did this because, even in the middle of a confusing Old Testament story that confounds our twenty-first-century, Western way of thinking, God is good. God stepped in to let Hagar know that, even as he was asking her to do something hard and horrible—to return to mistreatment—he was good. And faithful. And at work not only in Hagar's life but in the rescue of humankind.

But Hagar had to *choose* to believe this. And she did. Hagar chose to believe not only that this was God himself speaking to her—that she wasn't hallucinating or hearing voices—but that God would be faithful. She accepted a hard life based on her choice to believe in the goodness of God.

She chose to believe it. And she was right to. In choosing to believe this, she also chose to live in a ready position—ready to notice God.

Last winter—at yet another peak of yet another "Are you there God? It's me Caryn" moments—I stopped by some snowy woods one afternoon. My heart, soul, mind, body, every last thing about me had had enough with financial stress. Enough of difficulties in our family.

So I headed to the woods. Trees and water—miracle workers always.

As I stomped along the snow-covered trail—stepping out of the way of the chatty dog-walking ladies and the slow-strolling older folks—I shot angry thoughts up to God. When I ended up alone on the trail, I muttered my angry prayers aloud. Once again, I was praying about my family's broken finances and my own broken spirit.

When I turned from our finances to face the brokenness of my own spirit, I had to face down every failing, every sinful tendency, every regret, every fear, and this aroused a demon who had lain dormant but now threatened to overtake me. As I recounted all this to God, I reminded him how many times I'd prayed. For protection. For healing. For better relationships. For *un*brokenness. And now, for my demons to be taken away, sucked out, sent somewhere else. But even as I prayed, I scolded God for how silent he'd been. How unfaithful—yet again.

When I finished my stomped-out litany of complaints, I said, "Can't you just once swoop in and *do something?* Help me!"

Then a thought came—so different in tone than my previous rants, so quiet, so peaceful: *Why don't you stop?*

At first I thought this had to do with my complaining. But then the crush of snow under my feet became deafening. I realized how far I'd walked and that I'd now come back full circle. Literally. Back to the bridge over Salt Creek that takes hikers from the front part of the forest preserve and back into the woods.

Again, I heard it: *Just stop.*

Oh.

So I stopped. Stopped stomping. On the bridge, I leaned over and watched the water. I remembered the last time I was here— in the fall, where my kids and I had played "Pooh Sticks." Chaperoning one of those preschool field trips, my youngest son had been unwilling to release his "perfect" stick into the water. But then I told him that his stick was also perfect for a beaver dam and that a beaver would find it floating and use it for his house. Fredrik tossed the stick right away. Since then, Fredrik had been collecting perfect sticks for "beebers." He couldn't wait to get back here to throw them in.

I smiled and thought, *I'll have to bring him back here.*

Then I looked over to the banks of the creek and saw the

tracks. Two sets. One set, molded into the weak ice from geese, probably. But I couldn't tell. Then the other set—otter-ish— marked the snow along the edge of the creek. I followed them up the bank and through a hollowed-out log, but then I got distracted by a bird. I had no idea what it was, but it repeated a coo-call. The thrill had me looking up at bare branches, looking back to myself at seven years old when I won my Brownie troop's "I Spy" badge for bird watching. All the other girls had trouble seeing the birds. But I didn't. I could see the birds just fine.

Was that when I first fell in love with trees and woods? I wondered. *When I first saw and sensed how wonderful it was to just look at them? But why hadn't I looked for birds more since then?*

I was still focused on the noisy bird when I saw the falcon. Swooping. Across the bright sky above the pond just off the creek. I smiled. And mouthed, "Thank you." To my God, who it seemed had in fact come swooping in. Then I remembered this idea I'd had—the one about being able to use our senses to notice God—and I thought, as long as God was being show-off-y with the swooping in, maybe I'd put my idea to the test.

Behind the swoop was the sun. In the middle of the most dreary January I could remember, the sun glowed its yolky goodness, making the snow sparkle below. But better than the yolk or the sparkle that day was the warmth. I lifted my face and stood still, my face feeling sun-warmed for the first time in months. I breathed deep and smelled the crisp. Smelled winter. Smelled the God who creates such beauty in the midst of death and despair. The God who lets us linger at the brink but then lets us seek and find him in the woods. The God who sometimes takes away so that we can see more clearly.

Without the snow, without lush leaves, I could see the bird. Without snow collecting stamped tracks, so much goes unnoticed. Without it, it's hard to realize how much life exists in these woods, how much wonder.

Okay, God, I thought. *You've hit every sense—except one.*

I looked at the tracked-up snow, wondering if I was going to have to taste some—hoping I wouldn't. I didn't. Mostly because a lady and her Rottweiler passed by, and I wanted to pet the dog. She and I chatted for a moment. About how great Rottweilers were and how much I missed my dead one. About how beautiful the day was. About how the sun felt almost warm. She had worked up a sweat on the trail, she said.

After she left, I decided maybe four out of five senses was enough. I could assume that God could be tasted. He didn't have to prove it. So I turned off the bridge and headed back toward the parking lot when I saw it: a little sign pointing toward the red pump drinking fountain that was hidden in the trees. "TASTE," it said in big letters. With smaller words below, it warned of all the things one *shouldn't* taste in the woods.

I half expected the falcon to swoop again like an exclamation point from God. It didn't, and it didn't need to. I got it.

In a matter of moments, God had used my memories, my senses and other people to be present to me. Although he wasn't answering prayers the way I longed for, he was near. He was there. He was Emmanuel, God with me, training me to stay keen for him, aware of him, in all the broken bits and snowy paths of this life, reminding me that he'd been there and been present my whole life. And that, once again, I could find him and find him good.

Bread

The ten of us sat—some in sofas, some in cushy chairs, a couple on the floor—in front of the big stone fireplace. We were a "small group," brought together by church and life circumstance and a desire to study the Bible and discuss life "in community," as we say. Each of the five couples had been married several years, we'd each had a child—or had one on the way—and each held mortgages and good jobs to pay for them. Our lives were awash in the riches of suburban middle-class, American Christendom.

And that night, we read the prayer Jesus taught us to pray:

Our Father in heaven,
hallowed be your name,
    your kingdom come,
your will be done,
    on earth as it is in heaven.
Give us today our daily bread.
And forgive us our debts,
    as we also have forgiven our debtors.
And lead us not into temptation,
    but deliver us from the evil one. (Matthew 6:9-13)

As we worked our way through it, we discussed how little

of it any one of us really understood (kingdom come?) and how difficult it was to pray parts of it (God's will? not ours?). But then we landed on the bit about the bread, and I ended up confessing something. I told the group how, when I was in college, I lay awake one night thinking of the problem of homelessness, wondering how it happened, how a person could ever end up on the street. As it was at the time, I had three bedrooms—three beds—that were mine, that I could sleep in any given night: that one in my house at college, my bedroom back at home and my bedroom at my parents' lake house. Beyond that, I thought of the friends' spare bedrooms I could certainly crash in, the people I could call if every one of those three beds became unavailable.

I had realized back in college and I confessed it to the group then: my life of abundance had no room for understanding what praying for daily bread really meant.

Of course, others in the group tried to comfort me, shared how Jesus meant it *figuratively*. That Jesus really was telling us how to ask for whatever we needed to make it through the day. Daily bread, they offered, could be patience, endurance, energy, love, wisdom. It didn't have to be *actual* bread.

While I'm not one to take the Bible ridiculously literally, I couldn't shake what Jesus *actually* said. While the man was known to spin a figurative yarn from time to time, could it really have been that his prayer was tailored for rich Americans two thousand years later and that "daily bread" really only meant "*whatever* it takes to make it through the day"?

Maybe. But I wanted to know. So that night, while nursing my infant son to sleep, I prayed: "God help me understand what 'daily bread' is. Help me to know what you mean. And what it is we're really asking for."

Dumbest prayer I ever prayed.

My eyes welled up. I wondered if I'd need to pull over, hang out on the side of the expressway for a bit until I could see clearer.

Jesus, please, I prayed—not even sure what for: To dry my tears, yes. To keep me safe, sure. To provide, definitely.

A groan welled up from some place deep. I hoped God could hear it and that he knew how to speak Groan. And then my husband's words came to me again: "Better not write a check tonight," he said as I left for the banquet—the one I was expected to offer a donation at. "Shouldn't really use the card either."

While he'd given these warnings before—through the years of our financial crunch—he'd never said them in this context, not about giving. And I knew what these words meant this time: we were out of money. And not just out until next week or until the next paycheck. It wasn't until we could move a bit of money around as we'd done throughout the years, out of retirement savings into regular savings, perhaps. This time, we were out. We were done. The difficult business years and my unsteady freelance- and book-writing income had caught up with us, grabbed us, turned us upside down and shook us loose, our pockets dry. The savings accounts we had relied on while my husband shuttered his business and looked for full-time work and the money from my book advances and freelance gigs had gotten sucked up into the expenses of life. Gone.

So that night—on my way out to a benefit to help the homeless, a benefit where the powerful and wealthy gathered to support Breakthrough Urban Ministries, a organization founded years ago by my friend—I would have no money to donate to at least cover my own food, and certainly no money to help feed anyone else.

Seventeen years after lying in one of my three beds, smugly

wondering how anyone could ever end up homeless, and nearly ten years after asking God to show me what he meant by "daily bread," now I was much closer to knowing. Lucky me.

As I pulled into the parking garage I whispered a prayer of thanksgiving for drying my eyes so I could see. "But," I added pulling into my spot, "that's about it, God. You've really got to do better on this other stuff. You've really got to pony up."

The thing about attending fundraisers for the homeless is that you have to be some kind of fresh jerk to stay mad at God or lost in self-pity very long. It's hard to wander through a lobby full of displays of the work God is doing through an amazing ministry to change people's lives and *not* be able to declare that God is up to some huge things in this world. It's nearly impossible to believe that God may be at work in the lives of all the rest of the thousand people attending the event and in the lives of the thousands who are helped by the ministry every year but that he doesn't give a whip about you.

And yet, that night, I managed to do it.

I slunked my jerky self around the lobby, looking for the friend I was meeting—or any familiar face in the crowd. And found none. So I hightailed it to the bathroom, peed, washed my hands, brushed my hair and fixed my lipstick. I made small talk with the woman at the sink next to me.

"Don't you love this night?" she asked.

"I do," I lied.

"You been down to Breakthrough?" she asked.

"I have. You?"

"Used to live there," she said.

I stopped drying my hands and looked straighter at her.

"Wow," I said. "Amazing. And now you're back at the banquet?"

"Mmm-hmmm," she said and grabbed my hand. "God is so good."

I smiled at her. As she walked out, my smiled dropped. *Well, he is to you, maybe.*

Then my phone buzzed: a text from my friend telling me she was running late. *Figures*, I moaned heavenward. Since they were flashing the lobby lights, calling banqueters into the ballroom for dinner, I'd have to sit at a table full of strangers—alone—till my friend arrived. As any raging introvert can attest, this was pretty much my worst nightmare. A terrible night only getting worse.

As I weaved my way through the crowd and the rounds of tables, looking for the number that matched the one on my card, I continued my silent rant. *Way to go, God. Thanks a lot. You've really outdone yourself tonight. No money. No friend. No nothing.*

I reminded God that *giving* was my top spiritual gift. Reminded him that back when we had oodles of cash, we helped people. That if we had it again, I'd be able to help *these* people, help more women like the one I just met in the bathroom. That unlike some people who hoarded or carelessly spent their money, I *loved* to share it. So I reminded God how silly he was, how foolish. Then I pressed: *Aren't there enough homeless people, God? Do you really want my family on the streets too? Can you throw us a bone, God? A little freaking daily bread?*

But I didn't leave God time to answer. We'd have to talk more later. I'd found my table. Now was the time for small talk with strangers, to pretend all was fine, all was right with the world, and that God indeed was good. So I approached the strangers at my table with my full, friendly smile in place and set my purse down on a chair. After shaking hands and exchanging names and pleasantries, I sat. Then Ed, the man to my left, reached for the basket in front of him and held it out to me.

"Bread?" he asked.

The thing I didn't know—couldn't have known—that night was that praying for daily bread is not so much about receiving the actual *thing* we need. It's not about the bread—even when it *is* about the bread. It's not about the money or the stamina or the wisdom or the love we may lack.

It's hard to believe this when you need the bread so badly, of course. All those months that we depended on God and his people (our family members, friends, random people from church) to help us pay bills, to feed our family, to buy medicine and to pay for Internet, I thought it really was about the *things* being provided. After all, without the money others gave us while we looked for more work, we'd have lost our home. Not been on the street, probably, but crammed into a room at my mom's or my in-laws', certainly. I'm not sure where our dog or the hermit crabs or tankfuls of fish would've fit in. So every month that God did provide, that he did prove faithful through the generosity of others, I thought I was learning the right thing.

But I was wrong.

That God is Jehovah Jireh, my provider. That he shows up, like Ed with a basket of bread, isn't about our *needs* but about our *God*. And the miracle in all this isn't that suddenly we have bread or money or wisdom when just yesterday we had none, but that our high and holy God stoops low and lowly, that he enters our space to provide.

What I learned about asking God to give us this day our daily bread is that it's really asking God into our lives, asking God to be made manifest in our needs. Because when we learn to live—or are forced to live, as the case was for me and for so many of us—in ways in which we are dependent on God for the most basic of needs, when each morning we wake up wondering just how he would provide, we learn to look for his provision. So when we live asking for daily bread, we also live looking for it. And we see God every time a need is met. There is no such thing as coincidence in the daily-bread-dependent life. It's all from God's hand. And God's hand becomes very near and very clear every time we munch on our manna. And all that his hand touches and all the sweet space it reaches out over becomes holy ground.

God gets creative. That's the other thing in this. We know that God is creative, of course, because he is our *Creator.* But I don't think we really get what it means that God is creative until we become crazy, needy and desperate—for the material things of this world and for Jehovah Jireh himself. Because we so often miss his creativity—lived out through his people—until then.

I certainly didn't notice—not until the day my daughter and I needed a snack and we had no snacks, that is. The reason we didn't have snacks had nothing to do with our financial mess. At least not that day. Because the boys in the family were sick, the girls were just recovering and I was behind on a deadline, I wasn't going to send my six-year-old off to the grocery store with my debit card, no matter how much she begged, to get the cookies and the graham crackers and the yogurt and all the other stuff we run to in the middle of the day.

So instead, Greta and I stood in front of the open fridge doors and decided to "get creative." She pulled out a bag of flour tortillas. I grabbed the butter.

"Got an idea," I said and turned to the spice cabinet, reaching for the cinnamon.

Greta nodded and we went to quick work: mixing a bit of the cinnamon and some sugar in a tiny glass bowl, spreading the butter over the tortilla, and then sprinkling the cinnamon-sugar over all of it. We rolled it up and popped it in the toaster over— just long enough to let the butter and cinnamon-sugar mixture melt and mingle.

We cut our cinnamon-rolled tortilla into shareable bits, toasted one another, and bit in. I'd love to report that Greta and I closed our eyes, and mmmm-ed like crazy, declaring this the *best snack ever.* But we didn't. We just sort of shrugged and declared them *not bad.* Then we got glasses of milk to wash them down and talked a bit about the mighty tortilla.

"You can do a lot with them," Greta said. And right she was.

While I've never studied the culinary arts, and while I know virtually nothing about the anthropology of food, I love to *eat* a wide-enough variety of food to have paid enough attention to understand that the great foods of any culture tend to be born out of cash-poor-ness, out of neediness, out of desperation, perhaps. It's food intended to make a lot out of a bunch of little. And the flour tortilla is a classic example. Cheap and easy to make. Incredibly versatile, as they can be stuffed and layered and slathered and sprinkled, and their taste changes accordingly.

The Well-Filled Tortilla—the very first cookbook I ever bought—says, "When Europeans discovered the New World, they expected to find gold. Instead they found the tortilla."

"Tortillas," the authors write later, "*are* gold."

Certainly they are. And certainly they were to the families

throughout history who relied on them to stretch the small bits of meat and cheese and veggies and spices they had, and turned them into magical, sustaining meals. The same can be said for any culture's breads that hold slices of meat and cheese, and of the eggs that fluff up along with bits of ham or asparagus or mushrooms or sweet plantains, and of the rice that offers a canvas for the world's flavors to be dished on.

Each of these cultural staples *is* gold—and each is a sign of God's creative provision to us. Specifically, of the ways God allows *desperation* to breed creativity right in our literal daily bread. It's that creativity that launched a bazillion recipes. It's what allowed someone to see a black-shelled, creeping, crawling lobster and think, *Let's crack that sucker open!* It's what reached under the first chicken and what broke and scrambled the first egg, what sliced through the first pokey pineapple, and what faced down the fires of a habanero and thought, *We can work with that.*

But getting to this place requires hunger—the desperate sort that allows us to see options all around that once upon a time we'd have not considered. So it is with God and us. When we aren't desperate, we aren't looking. And we aren't noticing God or how he provides. And we miss a whole lot of holy ground. We miss a whole lot of what God is offering us through our needs for him.

My friend arrived at our table as I slathered the butter on the bread Ed had offered me. My mood had improved remarkably as it always does when God smacks me over the head and reminds me that he's got me. We chatted our way through salads and roast beef and potatoes and ice cream. And then we turned our chairs toward the stage where we'd hear plans for the ministry, hear what God was doing with every dollar donated and watch inspirational videos—including one by "Amazing Grace," sharing the story she wrote in a writers group I'd help lead. Then Heather Headley got up to sing. She sang many songs—all wonderfully, I'm sure. But I don't remember more than the one.

Headley said she hadn't planned on singing it that night, but she had heard this song on the radio recently and knew she had to sing it that night. As the music for Laura Story's "Blessings" began, I clutched the sides of my chair—knowing what was coming. It was one of the few songs played on Christian radio that I didn't switch away from—but, instead, turned up. I can't hear the words about "mercies in disguise" without tearing up. But while I was ready to cry again—for the umpteenth time that night—I wasn't ready to see my friend's shoulders shaking in front of me. Being the fresh jerk I'd already proved myself to be, I had assumed I'd be the only one crying. After all, who else here was out of money completely? Who else in that room knew the kind of stress I was living with? Who else here felt so abandoned by God—once again?

Apparently, from the tears around the room, lots of folks.

While certainly not everyone was dealing with financial stresses, seeing the tears around the room as Headley sang "What if the greatest disappointments / Or the aching of this life / Is the revealing of a greater thirst / This world can't satisfy"[1] showed me that everyone, everyone, has some daily bread they are desperate for—that only God can provide.

My small-group friends were right that night—of course daily bread isn't about actual bread. Not always, at least. It is about whatever we need to make it through the day, that thirst we have that only God can quench. For whatever reason, God took me through a time when actual bread was harder to come by than it ever has been again, when I got to experience his creativity and his provision and his love. But still, the sweetest thing he gave me during this desperate time was his showing up, being there, offering to walk with me, carry me, sustain me every single day.

I've never known a harder time of life, and yet I've never known a sweeter one, one where the ground glows holy. While I'm hoping that daily bread isn't so literal for me anytime soon, I don't want my daily bread life to end. I want to need something desperately every day that only God can provide. I want what Jonathan Martin calls "the truer luxury of needing God and believing He could do anything."[2]

And I think this is what Jesus meant when he asked us to pray the Lord's Prayer. Yet we can't deny the importance of the bread itself. Not if we believe Matthew 26:26, which says, "While they were eating, Jesus took bread, and when he had given thanks, he broke it and gave it to his disciples, saying, 'Take and eat; this is my body.'"

Though Jesus also says we cannot live by bread alone (Matthew 4:4), clearly "bread" has an important part in the Christian life. This Bread becomes what we need for this life—and the next. This Bread offers us fresh hope and fresh starts, beckons us— longs for us—to seek it every day. And when we do, we find him right there in it, and we find him good.

3

Mysteries

There are only so many times, so many ways you can ask God for rescue. When it doesn't come—at least, not like you want—you start to feel a bit foolish when you keep on asking. So after months (years) of praying that God would save my husband's business (and save us from the grief that went along with "failure"), that God would allow us to crawl out of debt, that he would provide well-paying jobs, that he would make tens (or hundreds) of thousands of people buy my books—and having the response be a continued sagging business, ever-sinking debt, no jobs and not enough book buyers—my prayers took a different turn. When I could pray, at least.

My prayers turned from "help" to "why?" I wanted to know why there'd been so many near misses when it came to jobs for my husband. Why he'd get so far in the interview queue and all would seem so perfect, and then nothing would come. I wanted to know why God had so many opportunities to help us clear our debt and he didn't. I wanted to know why God gave me the spiritual gift of giving and left us with no money to give. I wanted to know why he let us linger. Why he left us in this financial wilderness. Why? Why? Why?

And though I believe God wants us to come to him with our

cries for help, as I changed my prayer posture from pleading to seeking, something shifted. Begging God had left me cold toward him when he didn't "come through." It left me face down, distant, antagonistic. But somehow, questioning God drew me nearer, forced me to look at him as I sought answers. Not that I got all the answers, not that I should. But in this process of asking why, God revealed his mysterious, intriguing, irresistible self to ever-curious me.

The truth is, the *why* of faith has always been essential. I've been blessed to grow up in a faith tradition that welcomes questions, and because of this, my heart breaks when I read stories of folks who have grown up in churches where doubt was seen as sin and questions as rebellion. One of the reasons my Catholic-raised husband wanted to join the church I grew up in when we married and were church shopping was that my pastor assured him that this church didn't want anyone "leaving their brains at the door" on Sunday mornings. And indeed this "thinking church" has given me a safe place to come with questions and push-backs, as I seek to grow closer to God and become more Jesus-y. My faith tradition has stoked the fires of my curiosity and helped me embrace the mysteries of God and this crazy faith.

Though, once upon a time, back when I was seven and my parents were looking for a new church home, I'd never have guessed this white-bread, suburban Christian Reformed Church of hard-working, practical-minded Dutch folks would help me embrace the mystery and intrigue of God. After all, a different faith tradition gave me my first clues.

In fact, in the midst of their church shopping, had my parents asked seven-year-old me which church we should attend, there would've been no hesitation: Visitation Catholic Church. The reasons were simple, really: (1) I'd have gotten a dress for my First Communion—a frothy white one like my friend Lisa had. I wouldn't have had to "settle" for the lovely layered sky blue number that I wore to her party. (2) I'd have gotten a party. And all those envelopes full of cash and all those boxes filled with cross necklaces and red rosary beads. (3) My friend Lisa went to Visitation, so we could've sat together. And (4), I just knew we'd get to sing songs like the one my other friend Christy taught me: "Pray for the dead and the dead will pray for you."

The day Christy first sang the song—sad and slow, to the tune of Chopin's "Funeral March"[1]—I made her stop, then sing it again, even slower, so I could sing it with her. As I mouthed the words, my little religious world got rocked. I'd only just started believing in God; I'd only just accepted Jesus "into my heart." And yet, from the way things had been told to me, I thought I knew it all. Knew everything I needed to: God created the world. Adam and Eve (though mostly Eve, it seemed) sinned. But God loved us so much that he sent Jesus to die for our sins. If we believed all this, we'd go to heaven. If we didn't, well, we went to hell. End of story.

But the words to this creepy song that we sung again and again—now to a little dance-step we choreographed on the steps outside my grade school—plucked the strings of my mind, made me wonder if I knew anything at all. I mean, *Pray for the dead? The dead pray for us? There's a church that teaches this?*[2] *Why are we not there?!*

Perhaps some little girls would've been terrified by this notion, would've run screaming and crying back home, would've had nightmares for the rest of their lives about this sort of song, but not this little girl. I needed to know more. I wanted to know why

I hadn't heard of this, why I wasn't praying for any dead people. Why—for goodness' sake—we weren't Catholic.

When I rushed in the door after school, firing all these questions at my mom, she was cool. Ready. Growing up, her best friends had all been Catholic too. She understood my dress dilemma. She remembered wanting the party. She even knew the song! So my mom explained purgatory, offering her disagreements with the notion of praying for dead people—and certainly about them praying for us. But she said simply at the end of it all, "There's so much we do not know about God and about our faith. It's not as easy as 'we're right, and they're wrong.' God is mysterious."

If I hadn't already prayed the "Sinner's Prayer"—alone in our tiny, crisscross-wallpapered powder room just off the family room—I'd have dropped to my knees right there. God was *mysterious*? I had no idea. I thought he was all figured out. This was wonderful news. I loved it. And I loved God more for it. Because if God were a mystery—and he were a mystery *on purpose*—that meant he beckoned to be explored.

When Karen and Tracey sat across from me at our monthly writers group meeting and flatly declared in unison that I was a "five," my eyebrows crunched. Come on. What? How could they identify me—and my Enneagram type—so quickly?

I said they couldn't know—not if I didn't.

"No," Tracey said. "You're a five."

Karen echoed: "Definitely a five."

While our group carried on, commenting on someone's manuscript, I Googled away.

As if they know. Please, I thought, as I read through the description of an Enneagram type five. My mind tallied up the descriptions:

This . . . yes, fine, sounds familiar.

That . . . okay, sure, that could be me.

The other thing . . . almost certainly me.

But when I got to this line—"Drawn to the dark"—I stopped cold. Definitely. Absolutely. One hundred percent me.

For good or for bad, I am drawn to the dark side of things. Always have been. So even then, as my friends chatted around me, as I smiled and faked conversation or accepted a refill on my glass of wine, my mind rewound and took me back to Louisville, Kentucky. Back to the giant, white, antebellum house my cousins lived in. The one with the two-story foyer that showcased the Goliath Christmas tree every year. The one with the grand, central staircase that split at the landing (the landing where my Kentucky cousins gathered at the window once when it had snowed at Christmas and marveled at the falling flakes) and spun two sets of stairs off into wings.

Although I loved those stairs, although I begged and pleaded for my family to live in a house with stairs like that, although I chased up and down them and stopped to look out the leaded glass window on the landing every chance I got, the stairs I longed for most were the ones I could never find. The ones in the attic. Not to be confused with the ones *to* the attic, mind you.

Although those stairs *were* hidden behind a solid, white, paneled door, I'd found them. Though those stairs didn't even try to be grand. They were, instead, some sort of dark, broken wood that led straight up to the dark, broken-wood-paneled attic, which two of my boy cousins shared as a room, and which, these two cousins told me, contained a secret door and a secret passage, which led to stairs that circled all the way down to the basement. Once upon a time, during some war, my cousins told me, these secret-passage stairs were used to hide the house slaves. Their ghosts still floated up and down those stairs, they said.

Of the three or so Christmases we spent in that house—before the real horrors happening there were revealed, and my aunt and cousins moved out—I'd walk with my hands pressed against those attic walls, trying to find a panel that gave, a knob that pushed or turned and unlocked this mystery. To no avail. I never found it.

My mother told me my cousins were teasing me. There was no such secret staircase. There were no such ghosts. But to this day, I believe there was and there were. Well, maybe. But I've stayed desperate to go back, to see. Even these thirty years later.

I might be embarrassed to admit all this if it weren't for one thing: whatever it is that draws me to the creepy is what initially drew me to God, and what still does.

Whatever compelled me to explore my cousins' attic— pressing my hands on every wall, hoping a secret door would give way—was the same impulse that compelled me to look for signs of the God I kept hearing about. It was, at age seven, the terrifying yet comforting realization that God on high heard me, way down below, that made me believe in him.

And it was God's mystery, his invisibility, his at-once imma- nence and transcendence that made me long to know him more.

It was, ultimately, this longing to know God more—to search him out, to discover his purpose, his intentions—that was behind my "why" prayers. And though I didn't (and still don't) understand all the reasons why God had let us suffer so financially or why some businesses are allowed to thrive and others to stumble, simply by asking the question "why?" of God meant I was entering his mystery, seeking to discover the secrets behind what was going on—like I was back in my cousins' attic.

At this point, my love of the ooky-spooky, unknown and mysterious took over. I was hooked—reminded once again of how mysteries compel. Secrets and unknowns pique our curiosity, send us on quests and investigations, raise red flags and doubts, launch us into relationships and conversations. And while holding onto the idea that God is indeed good (certainly some days this idea was much harder to hold onto than others!), when I followed these clues and asked why, I chose to open my mind to the possibilities of what he was up to. To allow my intellect to seek him, to sniff out the clues of his goodness.

During my time of praying "why" I began to read mystery novels again in earnest. I'd been a huge Agatha Christie and Dorothy Sayers fan in earlier years and had devoured those books in the course of my reading life. But recently, I'd gotten lost in contemporary fiction and rereading English classics and hadn't read a mystery in years. Two random mentions of mysteries (Peter Lovesey's Peter Diamond series and Spencer Quinn's Chet and Bernie Mysteries) got me hooked on mystery novels again. And, somewhere in the midst of Peter Lovesey's *Bloodhounds,* the words "think different" came to mind. Mostly, I suppose, because one learns through reading mysteries that to crack a case requires one to think different. The run-of-the-mill and the obvious usually don't cut it (not sure if this is at all true in real-life crime fighting).

The phrase lingered long after I closed the book and went on to another. It seeped into my everyday life—in the way I parented, in the way I wife-d, in the way I wrote and edited, in the way I read, in the way I talked to friends, and in the way I communicated with God and "heard" answers to my whys.

It first happened when reading a feminist critique of God. The critique said God obviously viewed girls as dirty since the law in Leviticus declared women unclean for twice as long after giving birth to a girl than the woman was after giving birth to a boy (Leviticus 12:1-5). I admit, this sort of passage was one of the many that has long troubled me as well (not that I spend much time in Leviticus, mind you).

But as I read the critique and the verses themselves, again, the phrase "think different" came to mind. And when I asked God why he would do this, why girls would be less clean, "think different" brushed through again. So I did. And something different came to me: *What if*, I wondered, *this wasn't because God thought girls were grosser but because he was sparing the women*. After all, a baby girl in those days would've been a huge disappointment, would've meant a husband would've been eager to start trying for a worthwhile child—a boy. As one who's given birth three times, I can attest that being "unclean" for longer is not a bad thing (if you know what I mean). Suddenly, this odd little verse became not all that bad. Because of different thinking.

While I confess that I have not been able to "think different" and explain away every last bit of Levitical law (so many questions for heaven, God!), the idea of thinking different has reshaped the way I view our financial mess and God's allowing us to linger here. In thinking different, in embracing the mystery of it all, God's drawn me closer and deeper as I seek to understand.

By thinking different, I came to believe that, in this mess, even as we flirted with bankruptcy, losing so much and feeling abandoned at times by God, it's been in the "why?" and then the "think different" that I've sniffed out the clues that led me to finding God and his goodness, his very riches and abundance so near.

As much as I long to know the answers to my "why" prayers, and as much as I long to understand what on earth and in heaven God is up to, I also know that if I knew every last thing about our circumstances, trusting God wouldn't require much, well, trust. I certainly wouldn't seek God in these troubles. And if I never questioned, never wondered, I wouldn't keep asking, growing.

This goes for all of us and stretches far beyond financial situations. Consider, really, if we never asked "why?" of God, or if we never needed to scrunch our eyebrows and tilt our heads at the oddities of his world. If we knew all along when dinosaurs showed up or just why narwhals had that huge, weird tooth, we'd never explore this world, never get to know God through his creation, this general revelation. We wouldn't compile questions for heaven, and we might be less interested in going there.

If God weren't Mystery, weren't the God of "secret things" (Deuteronomy 29:29), faith would be unnecessary. God would be dull. Not compelling. Not someone we would long to know or understand.

Instead, we are drawn into the presence and very goodness of God when we are drawn into his mystery.

My mom told me to stand still. But I—a grown thirty-something woman—couldn't. Like Pee-wee Herman bouncing outside the Alamo, asking when they would see the basement, I tapped my hands and feet and shifted my weight until my time finally came.

"Can we see the attic?" I asked.

"The attic? Uh, no. That's off limits."

While I am normally compliant, a good, rule-abiding firstborn, this answer did not work for me. I smiled at the man, this dutiful park district employee, and realized I'd have to take drastic measures. After all, the whole reason I showed up for that day's tour—this "last chance to see the library before half of it gets razed and it gets returned to its former mansion-y glory"—was to see the attic. This attic that had been roped off for its entire life as a library. This attic that had tormented me for my thirty-something years of coming to this library. This attic that had reached down and teased me with its swooping, cream railing and its lush, carpeted stairs, as I'd creak past the landing to reach the periodicals.

True, the guide had already been gracious enough to take us into the bowels of the building, into a dank basement I didn't know had existed. He'd let us wander through back offices that had held minimal interest. And he let us take pictures of the places we'd loved best (for me, the open picture-book stacks where, at five, I'd sit cross-legged and run my fingers across the spines, trying to find Sendak). But none of that was what I came for.

I needed to know, needed to see, needed to understand what I (a library-card-holder and a taxpayer, mind you) had been kept from all those years. So I pulled out all the stops and did something shameful: I flirted. In front of God and my mother.

When the crowd had dispersed to take last pokes around the shelves and offices, I approached our tour guide again, placed a hand on his arm.

"Sir," I began, smiling gently. "Here's the thing: I've been wanting to see that attic my whole life. Is there any way you can make that happen for me?"

I put my hand to my chest and—God help me—lowered my chin, raised my eyebrows. I'd read that Princess Diana mastered this "have mercy" look. I may have batted my eyelids.

Our tour guide looked around a bit. I continued. "I understand liability issues and so on, but perhaps there's a waiver we could sign? I mean, you're the one in charge here, right? You *can* make this call."

When he said, "All right," I'm pretty sure I told him he was my hero. It was that bad. But as the small group of us who "wanted to stay after and see the attic" headed up those stairs ("Careful, everyone. Watch your steps and your heads. We're really *not* supposed to do this."), my guilt dissipated. I don't think the ends justify the means, but sometimes, they come close—especially when you finally get to see what lies to the left of an attic landing, when you get to run your hands across walls you'd only once imagined, when you open doors and see wallpaper and peeling-off pin-ups from the turn-of-the-century, when these rooms were servants' quarters and then from when they were early offices.

I could have cried as I wandered through the attic. It was a lifelong mystery solved. After a lifetime of wondering, imagining, I now knew what was in the attic.

But here's the thing about mysteries, something I learned that day: even the solving of them leads to more questions. Even as I now knew *what* was up there, *what* it looked like, I wanted to know more of *who* had been there, *why, when*. The best answers lead to more questions.

So even as I've started to get glimpses and big or tiny understandings of *why* God allowed our time in relative poverty, these understandings lead to more questions for God, another "why?" for every one that gets answered. And I'm learning to like that, especially as I sense God sending me off searching, peeking under rocks, running up stairs when the ropes come off—even, finally, finding the secret hidden panels and winding down stairs in the dark. I like that God loves me enough to make our relationship this intriguing.

Children's book author Kate DiCamillo once posted this on her Facebook page next to a picture of a tiny china monkey: "This little monkey belonged to my mother when she was a kid. He is made of china. His arms and legs are hinged and he can stand on his own. He is half the size of my thumb. He is at least ninety years old, and so when I hold him in the palm of my hand, it is impossible for me not to think about everything that he has seen and heard. He knew my mother when she was a child. What secrets did she tell him? This, for me, is always how a story starts, with some strange combination of ache and wonder, with a question that I don't know how to answer, with a small mystery cupped in my hand."

And so it is with God and us, I think. Our stories with God start with that same strange combination of ache and wonder ("why?!?!?"), with the questions, with the unknowns, with the doubts, with the mystery. Whether that ache and wonder sets us on a path or simply starts us spinning in place, noticing what's around us, it's what ushers us onto holy ground. In fact, every time we go back to the Bible, every time we read a theologian's work, or sit in our pastor's office, or pipe up at Bible study, or pray for clarity, or ask our moms or friends or neighbors what *they* think or believe about one of these great mysteries of our faith, we step into a space where God stands ready—in his time—to reveal yet another bit, a new angle, a fresh understanding. And in that place, we can find God and find him good.

4

Big Fish

The watch hit the carpet with a thud. I watched it fall, whipped off my wrist with the jerky movement of my arm. As it flew through the air, past the laundry basket on my bed, past the piles of clothes across it, I thought, *If only I were on a bridge*. Because, if I'd been on a bridge, the watch would've landed in a river below and been lost forever, a loss covered by insurance. A financial boon. But I knew better. The watch hadn't broken, the gold link hadn't finally worn down and given way, in order that I might gain financially. It wasn't like I had forgotten that moment, after all. The moment when my eyes had been drawn to the watch's shiny goldness and all it represented. So I knew: It had broken because I hadn't taken it off and given it away as I'd felt led, yet scared, to.

Years earlier, as my church kicked off a stewardship campaign to raise funds for our new building, my husband and I had pledged a hefty sum. A sum that, at the time, was perfectly in keeping with our high income and our belief that God would bless us financially. Then I had felt secure in my knowledge that God blessed us financially so that we could give. It was an exciting time—what with being so helpful to God and his kingdom.

But even as we pledged the amount and rejoiced in our ability to give so generously, I couldn't shake that there was something more I was meant to do. As I thought about it one Sunday, spacing out during a sermon, my eyes had wandered down to the watch. It had been a gift—a ridiculously expensive gift—from my parents for my high school graduation. Its solid gold band, crystal face and "oyster perpetual" state (where as long as my arm moved, the watch stayed wound) was the sort of watch meant to last a lifetime—and then some. The kind you pass down to children. It's what I had imagined.

And yet, it represented something more sinister in my life: my own desire to *be* rich and to be admired as rich. As well built and well-working as this watch was, really, it represented my materialism and my pride. My sin, in short. And I sensed that God was asking me to take it off, to sell it and to give the money away. But I didn't want to. I wanted to hang onto the memories, to the legacy, to the part of me it represented.

Every few months, I'd get the same sense. And I'd resist. When, not a year after we'd made our pledge to church, we had to call the finance committee and renege on our pledge because our finances had begun their drastic turn, I looked at the watch again. Selling it could benefit the church, I realized. But still. I resisted. Refused to go and do this thing I felt God wanted me to.

The week or so before my watch-flinging, I'd been reading my youngest son a children's book about Jonah, of Big Fish fame. He'd gotten the book from his preschool. As I read the story and tried to answer my preschooler's questions about how this could be, I confess that I was secretly rolling my eyes. I've nearly always been inclined to dismiss this Sunday-school staple.

Frankly, it's tied with Noah's ark as the Bible story I have the hardest time believing. Every time I read about dear old Jonah, I must remind myself that if I can believe in a risen Lord three (calendar) days in the grave, I can believe in a changed man after three days in the belly of a fish (right?).

But the day I read my boy that story, I didn't need so much reminding. Because more important than how many days or what fish, or probability or possibility, the theme of calling and obedience simply rang from the story. It rang loud enough that I grabbed an actual big-person Bible and read the text from Scripture. This time, I felt no need to roll my eyes. Certainly not at Jonah, who I had started to feel a kinship with. Something told me there was a Nineveh for me, and I was on the wrong ship, bringing about all kinds of disastrous waves.

When I bent to pick up my broken watch that next week, though I wanted to laugh or cry or something, instead I realized the watch had been a Nineveh, a calling I had ignored and disobeyed.

It wasn't that I felt God was punishing me, mind you. More like God was taking me up on my confessed desire to follow where he led. Less a view of a punitive God; more of a coach God, who's not afraid to push.

I believed this especially since giving away the watch wasn't my only Nineveh. There was another one lurking, another calling I had long ignored, one that God was using to start showing me just how seriously he takes obedience. Sometimes God uses big fish. Sometimes he uses financial crises. And not to discount free will, but let's face it—God is God. And when he wants a person to do something, he can get a person to do something, and when he wants a person in a place, God can get a person in a place. Especially when that person is like me, asking to be useful, praying to follow God's lead.

So here's the thing: for years I'd had the eensiest, weensiest inkling that maybe God wanted our kids to go to the local public school, instead of the Christian one we sent them to. This inkling at times manifested itself as a "fear" that we'd made the wrong choice,[1] and that God was going to make us change.

But like the stubborn Christian I always have been, I ignored the inklings, pushed the fears aside. I excused the faint whispers as just normal wondering. After all, why would God *not* want my kids at a Christian school? The one I had attended from fourth grade all the way through high school, the one that had shaped me for the good (mostly) and been so instrumental in my own faith? Clearly, that would be the place for them. Right?

Apparently not, because for every year I closed my ears to what I suspected was God's voice, that voice got louder. It got louder when the inklings became actual sentence-responses (*Maybe so they can become the people I created them to be,* God would whisper when I asked why they would need to leave). It got louder when I was asked to write an article about *why* I sent my kids to a Christian school and I ended up interviewing someone else since I could no longer come up with a reason beyond "because it's scary to switch schools." It got still louder when I found myself sitting in school board meetings—as a school board *member*—feeling like I did not fit. It got a lot louder when I saw the neighborhood kids go one way while my kids went the other, and that felt like a moral offense. And it got really, screaming-bloody-murder loud when my husband and I calculated the tuition for three kids at private school, and found, of course, we had exactly zero extra dollars to cover it.

So after three years of pushing aside an increasingly clear word from God, I emailed the local public school's principal. "I know it's not your job to sell the school or anything," I wrote. "But we're considering a switch and . . ." Though I decided to leave off the part about hearing from God, I wrote briefly of my fears and my questions. And then I hit send, knowing full well that this email would be a test of sorts for me. Even when emails have nothing to do with following God's voice, I put a lot of stock in email replies. I consider quick and thorough email replyers to be heroes among us. If not outright holy.

So when the principal emailed back five minutes later and included an invitation to meet and tour the school with my kids, as well as an encouraging word to me, telling me not to worry, not to fear, I took it as a sign—as a passed test.

But still, I'm stubborn. Or thorough, perhaps. And it came down to wanting to hear confirmation again through that simple whisper, the hush of the mind that rises up from a deeper spot than my scattered thoughts, that sinks its roots of wisdom deep into the spirit in my soul. I prayed throughout our principal-led tour the next week. *Here? Here? Is this where you want them?* As though our financial situation wasn't reason enough. I prayed it as we saw the old kindergarten room and the new, as we toured the labyrinth basement and the short-ceilinged art room. I prayed it as we passed plaques put up early in the last century, and as we walked through hallways built last year. I prayed up and down stairs. Waiting, listening. And then I saw the doors and heard the whisper.

The doors to Mr. Shepard's fifth-grade classroom are ridiculous. While, we learned, everyone tells him they are the prettiest in the district, I'd guess they are the prettiest in the history of school-dom. Two oak, double-doors, with windows paned in tiny squares. Above the doors, another window arches, something I imagine the morning sun can stream through.

I have a thing for doors, and these stopped me dead in my

tracks. As the principal and my family chatted with teachers who stood in the halls, I just stared and smiled. *Here?* I prayed again.

Here, God whispered.

Though I *thought* I heard a hushed *here* in front of a pair of beautiful doors, I couldn't be sure. Nor could I be certain it was really God who cut into my nervous prayer about a new school year with, *I've gone ahead! I've gone ahead of them and prepared the way!* Yet two months after hearing *here* and one month after hearing *I've gone ahead,* when our family showed up with a rush of neighborhood kids to check class lists posted outside, and when I scanned the lists for my fifth-grade son and saw his name on Mr. Shepard's list, I realized my boy would be a student behind those glorious doors and I knew: God had him in that place *(here!),* where God had gone ahead. Coincidence? Perhaps. And although I'm inclined to believe God speaks through coincidences, I'd even be willing to chalk it all up to odds at play. Four fifth-grade classes, one boy. Doesn't take a miracle to work that out. I'd be willing to chalk it up to chance, perhaps, were it not for Jonah.

Because after discovering my own personal Nineveh problem and my new kinship with Jonah, it seemed the guy turned up everywhere. Once, while doing some frantic second-guessing-our-decision-about-school cleaning, I found a Jonah picture book under our bed. Another time, while spaced out with worry, my youngest son sat down next to me and asked—out of the blue—if a fish could really swallow a person. Jonah became a little elbow nudge from God, reminding me he was there. And because I kept forgetting that God, indeed, had gone ahead,

Jonah kept popping back up. Like the morning I decided to Google my kids' teachers (don't judge: the snoopy journalist in me dies hard).

While there wasn't much to dig up—thankfully, no criminal pasts, no local scandals—Mr. Shepard did have one line in a bio on his church's website that left me a head-in-hands, weepy-delirious, overcome-by-God's-goodness-and-grace mess. "Fun fact," it read, "I've portrayed many characters in worship dramas and Vacation Bible School but am still remembered as the off-stage voice of the whale in Jonah's story."

When I finally did sell the watch—or to be honest, when I finally sent my *husband* to sell the watch (I couldn't do it)—we could no longer give the money away. We needed it. Had I listened to God earlier, the money might have gone to help another needy family or to pay for a few bricks at our church. As it was, we were the needy family it helped; our bricks were the ones it paid for. Not what God would've wanted most, perhaps, but in allowing it to snap free from my wrist and letting it bring home some cash, God's glory and wonder shined brighter than that watch ever could've.

Likewise, with the school switch: Had I listened earlier it would've been easier for my kids, less disruptive. But still. God's been so faithful and true, I can hardly stand it. He did, indeed, go before, and he is, indeed, using this to shape my children into the people they are meant to be. It's been wonderful, academically and socially, for my kids and, of course, spiritually for me. Perhaps also for them.

As many people tell us, we can know it's God's voice—whether from off-stage or from behind doors or while interrupting our prayers—when it aligns with Scripture. Yes. Obviously, the Voice of God is not going to instruct you to kill or to maim or to gossip or to act unloving toward your neighbor. But the Bible doesn't say much about school choices. Nor about many of the other things we fret over and that God may have a thought about for our lives—if we're asking. So I've learned that we can also know, can recognize, that voice when it leads to places of affirmation and confirmation in classroom placement and in silly facts about playing the Big Fish. We know that voice when following and obeying it leads to places of blessing—not always an *obvious* or *easy* blessing, mind you. God's voice led the Israelites to forty years in the desert. And God's voice led his beloved Son to the cross. Whether the "blessing" is immediate or delayed, whether obvious or obscure, we know it's God's voice calling and beckoning when suddenly we're deafened or calmed or energized or humbled by suddenly finding God there and finding him good.

5

Crosses

⤵

The Sunday before Ash Wednesday, I was tasked with getting ash. Our church was fresh out, and as a member of the worship staff, ash fell in my jurisdiction. But as a *new* member of the worship staff, I had no idea where I might procure said ash. I knew that some churches burned dried palm branches from the previous year's Palm Sunday, but I knew ours had historically not. So I imagined there was some other sanctified store or source where we got the ash.

Apparently not.

One thing I've learned from working in a church is how mundane much of it is—from the plastic pitcher I hold under the tap to fill the baptismal font to the Post-it notes I jot prayer and liturgy starts on. And yet, how the transformation from the ordinary to the holy is really the magic of church. While some have been undone by seeing behind this curtain, I love it. I love how ordinary, earthy folks use ordinary, earthy things to usher other ordinary, earthy folks into the presence of an extraordinary, heavenly God.

And the ash, as it turns out, is just about as earthy as it can get—since my boss's answer to my "where do I get ashes?" question was that I could either drive out to the Catholic supply store *or* I could build a fire.

"And just burn regular wood?" I asked.

"Yep," my boss said, before joking, "Though, actually, the more sinful things you can find to burn, the better."

My initial idea was to joke back, "Great, I'll burn my copy of *Fifty Shades of Grey* and my weed," but I thought better. We were standing in the sanctuary, surrounded by a few late-service lingerers who might not appreciate erotica and drug-abuse humor in the house of God. So instead I laughed and walked away. I'd burn logs, I figured. Like always. Maybe some newspaper for kindling.

As I drove home, I couldn't shake the idea of sinful things I could burn. I didn't actually have *Fifty Shades of Grey* or weed (not that *burning* those things would be the solution anyway . . .), but I wondered about my actual vices. Should I burn the cardboard case from my beloved case of Diet Coke? Or maybe the label from that bottle of pinot noir I drank, possibly a tad too quickly? What about the cork?

If this were junior high, I might've tossed in a couple of notes—gossip passed in the hallways. Or maybe a test—which, for one answer, I'd glanced at a neighbor's paper. Were it high school, I could've thrown in my *Cosmopolitan* magazines—though burning those glossy pages would be an environmental sin for sure.

By the time I pulled into my driveway, my boss's off-handed, silly remark had turned into a mission: I would find sin to burn if it did me in. Turned out, being done in was not required. Finding the sin was easy. No sooner had I walked in our back door than did my eyes land on the pile of papers on our shredder. It was stacked with credit card offers—"0 percent interest!"— and old bank statements.

Then I knew: the sin I needed to burn wasn't of the gossip or cheating variety. It wasn't either of my liquid vices. I needed to burn—confess and hand over to God—my financial, or "stewardship," sins.

Because, though I do believe God has used our financial mess to break and rework me, I can't in all good conscience say God caused it. He didn't will it. I believe he allowed it; I believe he chose not to rescue us many times when he could've (and, frankly, I still wonder why). And while plenty of the circumstances that caused our financial breakdown—a terrible economy for one—were beyond our control, plenty were well within them. Plenty that we chose unwisely—even sinned—in.

God didn't, for instance, tell me to encourage my husband to keep at his business even when he was ready to let it go, years before we *had* to let it go. I did that on my own because I was afraid, because I had married a business owner and wanted to keep it that way. Nor did God, for instance, insist that we take that very, very modest spring-break trip to Kentucky to wander through caves and eat in small-town cafes simply because I "desperately" needed to get away. I'm pretty sure God can grant rest anywhere. But I needed Kentucky.

And though most of the credit card debt we had accumulated, even as our income dropped like a boulder in the ocean, was from paying for two of our three kids' hospital births ourselves (we didn't have maternity insurance) and from other medical expenses (we had a high-deductible plan), and while most of the credit card bills we tried to pay each month had little to do with the "typical" overspending one associates with credit card debt, still. Still. We made bad choices. I overindulged, spent money we didn't have—especially when it came to my kids. I sinned. I didn't respect my husband and his prompts from God as I should've. I didn't trust God as I should've.

And the stack of bank offers and old bills became the symbol of a sin I'd been too busy praying for rescue from to think about confessing.

So I gathered up the envelopes, removed any plastic and tore the paper into fourths. My son and I created a little mound in the fireplace and arranged the other kindling and logs accordingly. The fire caught and burned hot and gold with streaks of blue. The burning paper especially excited my son.

"We need more paper," he said.

I agreed but told him the caveat.

"Those are my sins burning there," I said. My boy rolled his eyes. "I've been greedy," I started to explain, but he interrupted me.

"Then let's add more sins," he said. "I'll write some down."

And off he went to list his sins on some paper to toss in. I called after him to bring a stack. I thought we could all get in on this.

I explained to my other kids what we were doing—that we were creating ashes for the Ash Wednesday service, and that since Ash Wednesday marks a day for us to come to God, lamenting or confessing and declaring our belief in a God who redeems our sin and our hurts and our frustrations, we were going to write those things down. So that they could be transformed into the smear of a cross.

"So other people are going to wear our sins?" my daughter asked.

"Yup."

"Do they know this?" my son asked.

"Nope."

"Cool."

And so that afternoon turned into a roaring, burning ConfessFest in my living room. Who knew confession could be so fun? I filled pages and pages with my sins. I listed my demons and tossed them into the flames. My kids did the same. Though my daughter made up elaborate sins—"the time I punched that guy"—and when I suggested she add "lying" to her list, she balked. But smiled. My oldest never let me see his list. He's catching on that Mama writes about this stuff, and it's wise to keep it between him and God. And my youngest treated the list more like wishes. All fine too.

Because no matter what we had on the list, we saw them disintegrate into ash. Ugly, choking, stinking ash that, when smudged across our foreheads, would become the most beautiful, breathtaking, dazzling symbol of our faith. With the ashen cross we wear the Christian paradox: that out of pain, sin, faithlessness and suffering comes the hope, promise, mercy and rebirth of the cross. The cross, the very intersection where, for me and all who know him, God has always been most present and most good—ever since I first understood the suffering gift of Emmanuel and the peace that comes from that gift.

"Does anyone here have the gift of speaking in tongues?" our teacher asked.

I grabbed the seat of my gray, metal folding chair and twisted my body around, pretty sure that I would see zero hands raised in the group of grade-schoolers around me, probably every one of whom would burst out giggling like I wanted to.

I was wrong. Every hand—but mine—shot into the air.

"Great, then. We're going to head over here where it's quiet. We have an interpreter here with us today."

And with that, every child—but me—who had tagged along with their parents to this woodsy church retreat scooted through the lines of chairs, out of the big, log-walled gathering space and into the side room. It was a narrow space with more chairs and more windows, overlooking some pines and then the lake. Or pond. Or whatever that body of water was.

The teacher gave me one last look and a smile, then she raised her eyebrows, tilted her head, "Not coming, then?"

I shook my head.

"All right, then. Just sit there. We won't be long."

To be fair: I'm sure the teacher meant well. First, for believing that all these children were actually gifted with the ability to speak in tongues, and second, for thinking it was fine to leave me all alone in that room. And I'm positive that this woman wasn't actually the Hollywood-sinister-but-peppy camp leader my memory has typecast her as, but alas, this is what happens when you leave the already lonely girl alone: her memory turns you into a monster.

When the monster, er, teacher clinked the door closed behind her, I turned back to the stone fireplace in front of me, trying not to cry, hoping my parents' class would let out soon so they could come rescue me. When the murmuring began in the side room, I looked over through the small windows into the room, to see tiny arms raised, mouths moving, and a couple boys punching each other and laughing. Where was their laughter when I needed it?

I sighed, turning back to the fireplace, no longer wanting to cry. A seven-year-old's rage and disgust now bubbled inside. Instead, I scanned the fireplace's smooth rocks, got lost in wondering how they fit and held together—until I noticed the cross. Small and simple, carved and wooden ("unfinished," my mother would've called it, because it wasn't stained), set in a green-block base. The contrast of that wood—in its natural finish and unnatural shape—against the smooth purple-gray stone and the deep rugged wood of the mantle made me smile, filled me with something. Something I couldn't explain. I wanted to get up and grab it. Stand on the broad stone hearth and reach toward the mantle for that cross, rub my fingers across the grain. But I'd been told to "sit there," so sit there I did.

But the *something* continued to stay with me, rose within me even. Surrounded me. Where moments before I'd fluctuated from feeling sad to appalled to outcast, as I focused on the cross, this *something* was different. Now I didn't feel alone or anxious or awkward. This something was peaceful. I was okay.

I wondered if this *something* was God—with me. It seemed unlikely. I mean, of all the places in that log building where God should've been cooking up some presence, it was in the room that I didn't go in. It was in that place where kids (the non-punching ones, at least) held up hands and prayed in languages unknown. It was in that place where, apparently, grade-schoolers received and expressed spiritual gifts that I never would. I turned to look at the room again, expecting to see flames or doves or papers flying—what with the windiness of the Spirit—but I didn't. By then, just the teacher talked.

When I glanced back again at that cross and felt that cool, calm Something wash down through me—from the top of my head to the tip of my toe—I knew. God might have been in the other room (I'm actually sure he was), but he was definitely there with me too. Cynical me. Curious me. Angry me. Lonely, shy me. And I sensed he was smiling at me. His beloved. The one—one of many—he sent his Son to die for. On that cross.

I had learned—at that same church that sent us to this retreat center—what the cross meant. It meant I was forgiven, made new. It meant I had eternal life. But from that moment on, the cross became something else: a sign of peace. Now I not only knew that God *heard* me but that he was *with* me. Next to me, even.

The cross meant that I was never alone. That I didn't have to be anxious. That I wasn't awkward or outcast (though I'd never cease to feel this way, especially at church). That I belonged—

with him. The cross became a sign of God's presence, of his love, of his goodness and mercy.

But I didn't understand—couldn't, at the time—how the cross became all that. I didn't get the brokenness and sorrow and suffering that *had* to be present at the cross for it to be so. And though I spent the next decades of my life in churches, I'm sure hearing sermon after sermon on this very thing, and although I spent time in churches and cathedrals, studying the great artistic renderings of the Stations of the Cross, it never registered. Not until my youngest son was born.

Although the epidural for my firstborn, my son, only half worked (either only on my right side, or left; I can't actually remember), and although his birth was harrowing enough that the nurse told me afterward that, "a hundred years ago, that would've killed you, sweetie," it never occurred to me that, with my third child, my pain-relief method of choice would not work *at all*.

I mean, the epidural I received during my daughter's birth worked so well that I called her delivery my Beverly Hills birth. Not only was there zero pain, but I had to be directed to push: I couldn't feel a thing. The pictures after Greta's birth confirm this: nary a hair on my head was out of place, nor a tired muscle on my face as I cuddled both her and her two-year-old brother on my hospital bed. Easy-peasy. Fancy, even. Hence: Beverly Hills.

So I could only assume that Greta's baby brother would come easy like that as well. What, with him being my third child in less than five years, my body being experienced and knowing what to do and all.

And yet, it was not to be. After being induced and having my water broken, the epidural never took. The pain came hard and often, and it lasted all day. I managed to breathe through contractions well enough, squeezing my husband's hand or a bedrail, as I puffed out breaths and counted in my head before relaxing and waiting for another contraction.

But when the pain shifted, becoming something else altogether, the sort that says *push*, I panicked. I couldn't remember how to breathe through "transitional" labor and during the pushing. It'd been five years since my first Lamaze class, and my Beverly Hills birth experience hadn't exactly spurred me to brush up on my breathing techniques. But then I remembered: I needed a "focal point." Focusing on something was key. I glanced around the room, desperate. The teak dresser. My nurse's scrubs. My maraschino-cherry-painted toenails. That coat tossed over the chair. None of them seemed right.

So as I felt that ever-urgent, searing need to push, in between throwing up in the bedpan Rafi held out for me and panting through contractions, I prayed: *God, give me something to focus on.*

The words that came were clearer than any I'd ever heard— from God, at least.

Focus on the cross.

Ah, yes. Good. I rescanned the room, confident—in this Adventist hospital with a photo of Jesus himself, arms wide open, greeting visitors off the elevators and into the maternity ward— that I would find a cross to focus on. Surely one must be hanging on the wall.

There were no crosses. Yet I heard it again: *Focus on the cross.*

I checked the necks of my doctor, the nurse. No cross pendants. I looked around for a Holy Bible, perhaps a cross on that. No such luck.

One last time: *Focus on the cross.*

Where? What cross, God?

And then I saw it. Perhaps it was the drugs they had injected into my IV when the epidural failed. Perhaps it was the pain itself. Perhaps it was both—bringing on this vision. For sure it was God. Because there, mid-air, just beyond where my maraschino toes curled off the edge of the bed, floated a cross. And on that cross writhed a bleeding and broken Man. Jesus. Panting. Gasping. There. With me.

And I focused on it, on him—and breathed and pushed. And the pain became something else entirely once again. So purposeful. So loving, so beautiful.

But I had known this about the pain from my other two births. Even when I couldn't *feel* the pain during Greta's birth, I understood that connection between love and pain that is evidenced during birth. What I didn't know—didn't realize—until I saw the vision so clearly of Jesus suffering, of his blood dripping right there in my delivery room, was the connection of that pain and love to the cross. Until then, I hadn't grasped the connection between the gore and the glory, the blood and the beauty. Until then, I hadn't understood at all what the cross really meant. For Jesus. Or for me.

It was in the days and weeks and months after my Fredrik was born, as I thought back to the vision I had seen, that I realized what holy ground I had been on when he was born. Not simply because birth is a miracle, nor only because God was present to me during that birth. But because, with this new image, this new vision of the cross, God gave me something new to focus on: reminding me that not only was Jesus present in our suffering but he was at work through it.

"The sacred and holy moments of life are somehow the most raw, the most human moments, aren't they?" so writes Sarah Styles Bessey in "Incarnation" for *A Deeper Story* blog, which, incidentally, she opens with this line: "If more women were pastors or preachers, we'd have a lot more sermons and books about the metaphors of birth and pregnancy connecting us to the story of God."[1]

I believe she is right on both counts. Though, whether or not you think women should be *preaching* their birth stories, I'm pretty sure we can agree that Christian women ought to be sharing their stories of sensing God in pregnancy and childbirth—because the Bible has so much to say about pregnancy and birth when it relates to God's story. Specifically God's *redemption* story. Specifically to our salvation.

Consider one of the weirdest passages in all of Scripture (and this is saying a lot, since there are so, so many weird ones). Paul's little note about how women will be "saved through childbearing" in 1 Timothy 2:15 is certainly one of the many troubling things the man has to say about women, no? It's one of the many, many (many, many, many) lines I've read of Paul's and asked, "Huh?" Because, of course, it makes no sense. At face value, it's heretical even. Women are *not* "saved" through childbearing any more than men are saved by their—um—role in baby-making. We are saved by the blood of Jesus Christ—not the blood of birth. We are saved by faith—not by works (including the good word of bearing children), as Paul himself tells the Ephesians (2:8-9).

And, of course, this verse riles up all sorts of debate (when it's talked about, which is not actually that often). When I've asked pastor friends to help me understand this, they've done their best but—honestly—only confused me more. All roads sort of lead to "Yes, this is weird." That, yes, but also, Bessey is right.

No matter what we believe these verses mean, giving birth—
with the pain and blood and gore and terror and struggle—may
not "save" women in a way synonymous with any "Sinner's
Prayer" experience nor in a slow-road-to-conversion way, but in
many ways, childbirth saved me.

Not because I wasn't already a Christian. Had I died the day
before birthin' my baby, I'd have gone to heaven. Nor did it save
me because I didn't seek to follow Jesus before Fredrik was born.
I did. Or, I tried. However, with Fredrik's birth, with my vision
of the cross and of Jesus writhing on it, I was saved in a new way.
I got a new understanding of the connection between love and
sacrifice, between suffering and salvation. And with a new understanding of what Jesus did for us because he loved us, I could
see more clearly what it means to take up a cross, and I could
see the good and transforming work that happens when our
pain leads us to the cross.

So, although Paul almost certainly didn't mean to, this
weird, confusing little verse offers an insight into the amazing,
redemptive gift that God offers women in the "curse" of
childbearing (see Genesis 3:16).[2] This is not the only way
humans can understand the cross, certainly, and there are
plenty of ways to understand the cross in this world that is
hobbled with hurts. But I believe this insight can give women
evidence of God's goodness and faithfulness. Of his ultimate
longing to redeem suffering, to redeem pain, to redeem
(save!) us.

Hear me out: Despite a dire consequence of Eve's sin—a
curse!—God still brought good from it (as he does with all pain
and consequences, really). And I don't just mean the good of a
baby. Eve's curse gets redeemed not only because her own childbearing (i.e., her lineage) led to the Savior but because women
"get" to suffer for our babies, to enter a bit into what Jesus suf-

fered for us, to understand the enormity of his love and the pain Jesus endured to bring forth life for us.

When my oldest son was nine months old, he went through a period of screaming every time I put him down for a nap. He'd fall asleep in my arms while nursing, but the second his head hit the crib mattress, he'd turn and wail. I took solace in Dr. Marc Weissbluth's *Healthy Sleep Habits, Happy Baby,* and when I noticed Dr. Weissbluth's offices were in Chicago, I took further solace in taking my son to see this amazing pediatrician and sleep specialist.

In fact, I credit the man with saving my sanity. Truly. At a time when I was convinced I was the worst, know-nothing mama on the planet, the kind doctor assured me otherwise. Dr. Weissbluth suggested many ways to help get my son sleeping better, but the biggest takeaway for me was a comment that shaped not only my motherhood but also my theology.

When discussing the whole controversial cry-it-out aspects of getting a child to sleep, Dr. Weissbluth (who believes babies over nine months old *should* "cry it out" for periods of time) reminded me there was a difference between "allowing a child to cry" and "making a child cry."

"There will be times, throughout your kids' entire lives, when they will cry," Dr. Weissbluth said. He told me there would be tears from tantrums, tears for getting in trouble, tears for hurt feelings and so on, and sometimes a mother's job would be to allow the tears for good reason. In this case, it was allowing tears so my son could learn to get himself to sleep.

Letting him cry it out the first time nearly killed me. But I let

him. And he fell asleep—fifty-nine minutes into the one hour Dr.
Weissbluth told me to give him. The next day, he cried less. Ten
years later, my son is the best-sleeping kid I know.

Of course, our mother hen of a God does the same thing. God
doesn't *make* us cry, but he allows it. In my head I know this. In
my heart, it's always difficult.

God didn't make our financial crisis, but he allowed us to cry
in it. And just as I allowed my son to cry, ignoring his pleas for
a crib-rescue so that he might have something better (sleep!), so
God allowed us to cry, ignoring my pleas for financial rescue so
I could have something better. This is the story of Jesus on the
cross as well. Crying out in Gethsemane for a rescue that didn't
come. Asking why he'd been forsaken as he hung, nails through
hands, chest heaved forward, blood and water and urine dripping
everywhere. Even at that cross—and in all our crosses—God is
at work. Even if, even when, he's allowing us to cry. And in that
place, we find God and we find him good.

6

The Goods

ᘒ

I had gotten used—if, I suppose, you can get used to charity—to unexpected financial gifts from family members. Once my husband shared a bit of our story and the direness of our situation, we were overwhelmed by generosity and love, which took the forms of "widows mites" to no-interest loans. But one particular bit of charity caught me off guard.

I held the stack in my hands, a pile of $100 gift cards for the local grocery store, and fought back tears. Not that long ago—at least, it didn't seem that long ago—the man who had sent these had talked with my husband about merging businesses, aligning their two individual, successful financial management companies into one. It didn't come to be. Even at that time, my husband sensed he needed a switch, knew that God had something different in store for him and that a merger would not be the right path.

But as I held the cards, I cried at how quickly things had changed. Just a few years prior, this man would've been a business partner. Today, he was our rescue. I reached for the cabinet where I kept my own stack of cards—thank-you notes. I had no idea where to begin or how to thank this man, didn't know which words could convey what this generous gift of grocery-store cards meant to us, to me. And yet, I needed to find something, some words, to let him know that his action—taken immediately after a lunch, where my husband told of letting his business go and of looking for a job—left me reeling with humility and gratitude, left me dizzy with God's presence and goodness, and left me feeling as though Jesus himself had sent the cards. Which of course, by appearing in the form of this good man, he had.

"Not good," the teacher said.

And we—a circle of fourteen-year-olds on one side of the church nursery, fighting for space next to cradles and ride-on trucks and rocking chairs—had gathered for our weekly Sunday-morning catechism instruction, and we rumbled our objections.

In 1986—the age of Farm Aid and Live Aid and Hands Across America—you could not tell a group of newly minted, freshly angst-ed teenagers that what these aid organizers had orches-trated, what we were jabbering about that morning in response to the Heidelberg Catechism's Day 3, Question 8, was *not* good. You could not tell us that it was "not of God," even if his name wasn't really invoked, and expect us to believe it. These events, these actions *were* good.

But our teacher read the question and answer again:

Q: But are we so corrupt that we are totally unable to do any good and inclined toward all evil?

A: Yes, unless we are born again, by the Spirit of God.

And our teacher snapped the book shut. End of story. End of discussion. Unless these musicians and organizers knew Jesus, our teacher told us, what they did, even how they tried to help, was "not good."

At fourteen, I refused to accept this. Just as when this same catechism teacher said a week later that it was also "not good" for girls to go to college because it was a "sin" for them to work, I refused to accept that. As did the elders of our church who, thankfully, promptly removed the teacher from instructing young minds. And thus ended my instruction in the catechism. I never got beyond Day 3. It would be more than twenty years before I would read the final forty-nine days.

And yet, those few weeks in that man's class have stayed with me. In fact, though I never completed catechism, four years later I would stand before that same congregation and profess my faith, promising to take on the church's joys and sufferings as my own. I publicly agreed with the doctrines and teachings and became a full-fledged member of a church that did, indeed, believe that we are inherently sinful, totally depraved.

I believe it still. It is but by the grace of God alone that we broken, sinful people are capable of good at all. It is but by the grace of God alone that this broken and fallen and full-of-death creation can still sparkle God's glory at every turn.

What I do *not* believe—what I disagree with in this quick Q&A—is that people must be "saved" to do good. The answer rightly says it is only through God's Spirit that we can do good, but it wrongly asserts God's Spirit only affects those who are "born again." As my church's lead pastor, Reverend Peter Semeyn, told me, it "seems to fly in the face of general grace. These wickets stick."

Indeed it does. And indeed they do.

There are all sorts of reasons to disagree with this. *Total depravity* and its various sticky wickets have chopped through Christians and churches for decades. I can look at John 3:3-5, the passage the catechism authors cite to support their claim, and pick it apart (isn't being able to "*see* the kingdom of God" different from being able to *do* good? I think so).

But what has always driven me to disagree most strongly with this is less specifically theological: it's simply that if Christians are the only ones able to do good, any good of any sort, then it seems that we have to limit how we see God, how we see God's image reflected back toward us in one another, in the workings of our very flesh. It seems we have to limit how and when we see Jesus when we offer glasses of water or when we offer a sweater or when we offer a prison visit to another human being. For if they are not born again and, therefore, not good *at all*, then we cannot possibly see our good and perfect God—and yet, Jesus tells us the opposite.

I walked not ten feet behind her, my own stride lengthening and my own pace quickening so I could catch the "walkin' man" signal and make it to Mario's Pizza, just under the "L" tracks. Normally during a summer weekday in Chicago's Loop, lunchtime is busy, buzzing with enough bodies—feet clicking across hot sidewalks or bottoms resting on shady benches or against cement walls—that no one stands out much. But this woman, this woman I walked not ten feet behind, had caught my eye blocks back.

She was probably thirty (old, nearly) to my (then) twenty-two. She was beautiful—her sleek blond hair pulled back into a low ponytail that swished across the taupe of her jacket. But it was the way she moved—fluid yet angular, effortless but with purpose—that struck me. At one point, I looked around to see if she was being filmed. I would not have been surprised to see her strutting across my TV screen to the beat of a hair-care jingle.

But there were no cameras. It was just her, well-bred, put-together, "classy" and striking. I had been imagining her elegant life, her high-powered job, her cocktail parties and her yacht excursions when I saw her swoop, mid-street, and bend her knees. Her hips wiggled and knees knocked and flayed a bit as she caught her balance. Then I saw her elbows jut as her hands—her palms up—scooped at the ground, over which she now squatted. This pose would have to be edited out of the commercial.

But then I saw the gray and heard the coo. This woman had squatted to scoop a pigeon—a pigeon!—out of harm's way. My eyes widened as she straightened her skirted-and-pantyhosed legs and crossed to the other side, where she knelt, this time with knees together (this could go back in the commercial) and opened her hands. The pigeon—this filthy, city pigeon—hopped out, its left wing dragging a bit, and hopped forward along the sidewalk. The woman walked on—as if it never happened.

But it did. And I smiled the rest of the day remembering it. In fact, eighteen years later as I replay the moment, I smile still. Her simple act was one of the best things—the best *good* things—I've ever seen anyone do. Mostly, probably, because it was so unexpected, seemed so "out of character." But that's what made it so terrific. Out of this perfect, clean, glittering image comes a woman willing to stoop in a city street and scoop to rescue a flee-filled, feathered beast. I still have a hard time coming up with a better image of Jesus than that. She did good—and the image of God seeped through her skin and through that act.

Of course, I have no idea what her "faith walk" was. I have no idea if she'd been born again, if she had accepted Jesus into her heart, or if she was personally filled with the Holy Spirit. Maybe she was. I like to think that this is what every Christian would do: see a struggling bird (or a struggling anything or anyone) in the street and, never mind what they looked like or what germs they picked up, bend to help. But we don't. And this woman did. In her act I saw good. And I saw God.

I saw this good and this God again recently, in a video clip from WGN's *Morning News* show. On one of Chicago's 100-degree, humid-as-all-get-out, had-been-storming-so-we-lost-power summer days, the traffic helicopter caught sight of a loose poodle-mix running along the Stevenson Expressway (I-55). As car chases in L.A. capture our attention, so it goes for loose dogs in Chicago. (I'm quite proud of our interest in seeing lost dogs found.)

All the while, a man sat at home watching the story unfold on the news, watching cars slam on brakes and freeway traffic pile up, watching people throw open car doors and leap out trying to capture the dog, watching state police patrol cars creep along behind the dog on the shoulder. He watched until he heard that the dog on the loose was just blocks from his house. At that point, he leapt up, threw open his front door, dashed into his own car and went to find the dog. And find it he did!

He and another man ended up gathering the terrified dog—whose rear paw was dotted with broken glass, whose fur sat clumped and matted, whose body lay weak from exhaustion and dehydration—in a tangle of bushes and roadside scrub. When the men emerged triumphant with the dog, I saw—once again, without knowing their faith or their hearts—good. And I saw God.

Perhaps the catechism writers would argue that *seeing* good and *being* good aren't the same. Of course, for all I know, the pigeon-woman and the dog-man could've had the most evil motives ever. Perhaps the pigeon-woman only rescued the pigeon, only scooted it out of the street, so that she could head back to her office and change from her heels into steel-toed, pigeon-stomping boots. Perhaps the dog-man only rescued the dog so he could boil it up later that night and pair it with a nice Chianti.

Perhaps not. Probably not. Most likely, the Spirit of God is loosed enough on this planet, is so vigorously at work, that there's enough to pour over and move hearts toward good acts even if those same hearts don't recognize the Spirit or know or believe in any ultimate Source of good.

But, perhaps it depends on what one's definition of *good* is. If *good* means "righteousness, or some act that recognizes its source as from the Holy Spirit and repents of its imperfections," then perhaps those catechism writers are right after all. Only those who have been "born again" can do that sort of good.

However, if we're talking about good, old-fashioned *good,* as in a generally recognized human condition, as in something that the very good nature of God himself has allowed to spill out over every square inch of this world and its inhabitants, then they are wrong. Still.

And yet I'll give the catechism writers this: as Christians, we believe that *doing good* is not about us. It's not about our personal piety or our virtuousness or our high moral standing. Doing good is about serving others and pointing to God. Whether the do-gooder recognizes God in it or not.

Interestingly, the catechism writers use John 3:3-5 to support their troublesome answer to their can-we-do-good-without-God question:

> Jesus replied, "Very truly I tell you, no one can see the kingdom of God without being born again."

"How can anyone be born when they are old?" Nicodemus asked. "Surely they cannot enter a second time into
their mother's womb to be born!"

Jesus answered, "Very truly I tell you, no one can enter the
kingdom of God without being born of water and the Spirit.

What initially bothers me about this as a "proof" to their
answer is that the passage speaks nothing of do-gooder-isms, the
very thing the catechism asks. What this passage does, however,
is reveal a tricky little tête-à-tête between Jesus and Nicodemus,
who was a Pharisee and presumably a do-gooder, at least in that
strict, rule-follower sort of way. We don't read Jesus talking
about changes of heart, about desiring to *do* good deeds, but
instead, we see Jesus talking about how people can *see* the good
by recognizing the kingdom of God at hand.

So, assuming that the pigeon-saving woman wasn't going to
come back and stomp the thing, when she saved the pigeon that
woman may very well (and *should* very well) have felt good
about herself, may have smiled as she walked, patted herself on
the back as soon as she caught a private moment when elevator
doors closed in front of her. Certainly the pigeon she saved felt
good, as the beneficiary of her act of mercy. However, the Bible
passage above, the one that leads to that most famous verse in
John 3:16, seems to be less about the person doing the good or
about the feeling of the good. It's all about the people seeing the
good, as we are the witnesses of the good.

So I wonder if Jesus thinks the pigeon-woman's feelings or the
pigeon's feelings matter as much as the recognition that was God
at work, that his kingdom was right there, at the intersection of
Wells and Washington.

The writing prompt I offered was "the beautiful and the broken," and I gave everyone ten minutes to write. Free-flowing. Whatever came to mind as we considered the beauty that came from the broken in our lives. As we went around the tables, sharing what we'd written, the stories varied: some wrote about getting evicted from apartments; some wrote about losing loved ones; some wrote about worry over children who had wandered off into the world and had never come back; some wrote about addictions and rock bottoms and recoveries and relapses; some wrote about waiting for God (lots of us wrote about waiting for God).

Grace, however, wrote about being and seeing Jesus. She wrote about being raped and beaten in an alley by a man who had offered her drugs. About being stripped naked, then wrapped in a blue, plastic tarp and tossed in a truck where she stayed—for days—while her attacker drove around and around and around the city of Chicago. She wrote about being soaked with urine and feces in that trunk. About not being able to breathe. About crying out to a God she wasn't sure was there. And then she wrote about how she ended up at Breakthrough Urban Ministry's women's shelter, where my writers group met with theirs that night.

Her rapist—coming down from his high—came to his senses. When he remembered what he had done, he pulled over on a random street on Chicago's west side, in its notorious Garfield Park neighborhood. He popped open the trunk and found Grace, barely alive, and asked her what she needed.

"Water," was all she could say.

The man walked up to a door—the very door I had just walked through to lead this writer's group—the door to Breakthrough's women's shelter.

Grace got water and her release. Her rapist dropped her off blocks away. After a stay in the hospital and at another homeless shelter, Grace found her way back to Breakthrough, the place she *knew* she could find help and healing and hope and all the other things her life lacked. Because she knew it was where she could find Jesus.

When Arloa Sutter—Breakthrough's founder and executive director—asked her how she knew this, how Grace knew she'd find Jesus as Breakthrough, amid wide eyes and sniffles, Grace looked across at Arloa, shrugged and said, "When I was thirsty, you gave me something to drink" (see Matthew 25:35).

I love when a story, a concept, an idea, a long-held belief gets flipped on its head. And I love when God goes ahead and does this for us. Like he did with the story Grace wrote, titled aptly, "Amazing Grace." Because, of course, the way Jesus tells it in Matthew 25, Grace—bloody and pee-soaked and covered with her own crap—would've been Jesus.

In the story of the sheep and the goats, Jesus says:

> "For I was hungry and you gave me something to eat, I was thirsty and you gave me something to drink, I was a stranger and you invited me in, I needed clothes and you clothed me, I was sick and you looked after me, I was in prison and you came to visit me."
>
> Then the righteous will answer him, "Lord, when did we see you hungry and feed you, or thirsty and give you something to drink? When did we see you a stranger and invite you in, or needing clothes and clothe you? When did we see you sick or in prison and go to visit you?"
>
> The King will reply, "Truly I tell you, whatever you did for one of the least of these brothers and sisters of mine, you did for me." (Matthew 25:35-40)

Though I confess to cringing at Jesus calling anyone the "least," if ever a human is reduced to "least" status, she'd be a raped-and-beaten-and-left-for-dead woman (or man or child) in the trunk of a car. Hard to get much "less" than that, as far as humane treatment is concerned.

So Grace *is* Jesus. The person who gave her water (her rapist? the woman at the center? Arloa? Breakthrough's volunteers and donors? We don't know who it was) gave that water to Jesus Christ himself. This is how we understand it most of the time.

And yet, in that moment, Grace *saw* Jesus in that person's good act. God was all around, present and visible in everyone, and that bloody, horrible, wretched, crime-scene trunk of a car became holy ground.

It all gets back to how we see one another: *Who* we see reflected when a family member or near–business partner sends financial help. *Who* we see shining through when a debt is whisked away. *Whose* hand we believe is at work whenever we see good—whether the person knows they are doing it or not.

Because *how* we see ultimately shapes *whose* kingdom we see when we look around this world. Which is exactly the point of John 3:3-5. When we are "born again" in the Spirit of God, yes, it means we will someday enter God's heavenly kingdom, but it also means we can *see* God's kingdom right here on earth.

And while we can see it and feel it and smell and taste and hear it when we are on our own, stomping through woods or splashing in lakes or traipsing through deserts, we see it best when we see it in each other—no matter what sort of mess we're in. Because when we are Jesus to one another—when we are Jesus to pigeons and lost dogs and women locked in trunks—we shine light into the darkness, and we find God and we find God good.

7

Shocked

Z

The text buzzed my phone moments before my 5:30 a.m. alarm did. "Due to bad weather, school is canceled for today." I rolled my eyes just moments after opening them. *Closing school for a bit of rain?*

But then I remembered that I've been known to sleep through a storm or two in my life and that, although my town is one of the best in America—we have great schools, great parks, nature paths, wonderful people, stores and restaurants to walk to, a world-class library, our own symphony orchestra—we are not known for our ability to process rainwater. Or to keep the power on, for that matter.

So I thought I'd better check this "bad weather" out before getting too judgy with the school superintendent. I peeked out the window. Looked pretty wet. In fact, Lake Rivadeneira had returned in the south portion of our yard, seeping under and through our fence to join Lake Neighbor. I had managed a smile at the islands formed by mounds of mulch around our maple and crab tree when it hit me: *Crap. The basement.*

Two years earlier we'd flooded like crazy. More than two feet of rainwater backup killed our furnace, our carpet, our drywall, our dryer and more personal possessions than we could count.

We'd lost so much: my kids' artwork, stories I'd written in grade school, books, games—even if I did gain a great closing story for a book ("It's all copy," we writers like to say).

So with much fear and trepidation I opened the basement door and flicked on the light: déjà vu. *More* than two feet of rainwater backup. Although, we were smarter now, piling important stuff on high shelves, putting down removable (dryable?) area rugs instead of reinstalling carpet, letting the walls stay drywall-less, but still, water, water everywhere. Drum kits floating, along with guitars and amps and pianos and toys and bins of goodness-knows-what were underwater again.

For the second time in two years I sat on the steps and stared at Lake Basement. I hoped my rain boots were still in my bedroom closet and that I hadn't put those downstairs yet. I plotted how I'd rescue the drums and spied out other tubs of stuff that could float close enough for me to grab without getting electrocuted. I wondered, *Is the water really just rainwater—or is it something worse? How long will this take to drain, will the insurance come through again? Do they cover the same things twice in two years?* (They do.)

Though I would have a meltdown the following day—head held in hands as I cried, *Why us? Why again?* at the kitchen table before taking my kids to school—that day I felt nothing. No fear. No anger. No sadness. No nothing. Not because I'm so faithful and trusted that God would come through. I didn't feel that either. It was just a big, blessed nothing.

In the novel *When Will There Be Good News?* by Kate Atkinson, Dr. Joanna Hunter claims to remember nothing of her mysterious whereabouts for a few days because of a "dissociative fugue state." This is, the character says, "trauma brought on by the memory of a previous trauma."[1]

While a dissociative fugue is a rare psychiatric disorder, and while I certainly did not suffer from it sitting on those steps that day, the idea that "trauma" can be brought on by the memory of a previous trauma rings quite true for those who've walked through financial disasters. The unadulterated vulnerability of being broke makes the world a much scarier, more traumatic place. When you can't afford to fix a car or a heater or that cavity in your kid's tooth or when you can't replace or repair what's lost in a basement flood, stress lurks everywhere, ready to sink you in the rainwater. Or at least it did with me. Many times.

But there's something else that lurks during these times, something I learned to realize was not what we'd desire in these situations—but something from God nonetheless. It was something that took over my mind again that day on the steps, and it kept me going even when the fear or frustration or vulnerability would've been too much. It was something God has used to remind me that, when I am weak, he is strong. It was, when I came to recognize it, something like *shock*.

And the thing of going through shock is that it readies you. In horrible situations—physical, spiritual or emotional—shock replaces fear with this beautiful trust in your body, in your mind, in your soul and in your God. And in those moments on the steps, and throughout the day that followed, when there was little we could do except wait for the rain to stop and the waters to recede, I'd hear God speak into my shock and ask, *Who's got this?* And because I could not feel or think differently, my mind whispered back—on autopilot—*you do.*

We had just been trotting in the ring. I don't know what she saw or what spooked her. I just know that when she reared, my legs tightened, but not enough. I bounced forward, up and out of the saddle. Her nose, hard, long and white-striped brown, stopped me from flying over her head completely. Since this was just the week after Christopher Reeve's famous and disastrous fall from a horse, my trainer would tell me the horse saved my life—or at least my neck. Perhaps she did. Perhaps her head swinging back toward mine was an act of angelic intervention. However, as blood gushed from my own shattered nose, I wasn't quite ready to see it that way. But then again, in the moments after our faces collided, something switched in my brain.

I don't even remember it hurting. All I knew was that something was wrong—mostly from the blood that poured out and from the look on my trainer's face as she ran up beside me. But I settled back in the saddle, proud not to have fallen, and then I stood in the stirrups, swung a leg over, and dropped to the ground where my instructor ran a hand down my hair and thanked God it was just my nose.

"Since I didn't actually fall, you're not still going to make me get back in the saddle, are you?" I joked as Rafi (my then-boyfriend) ran up with my dog.

I ignored the troubled look on his face and began detailing the plan. We'd need to call my parents. Have them meet us at the hospital. They could take Gussy back to the cottage. *Did Indiana hospitals accept Illinois insurance cards?* I wanted to know.

Rafi assured me they did, as another woman brought me something to hold against the blood source.

Was I all right? Did I need to sit? everyone else asked.

I was fine. I just needed to leave, get into the car, to the hospital—once we found out where it was, at least.

As we walked out of the ring, past the stables that I could no longer smell and as we drove on toward the hospital, I continued a litany of directions and to-do's. Rafi would later tell me it was as if I broke my nose on horseback every day, such was my casualness.

I don't remember *feeling* anything at all. No pain, no nothing. Until we got to the hospital. And then, once we'd filled out forms, gotten the dog back with my parents, settled into waiting-room chairs, I realized that my nose would need to be *fixed* (*would they set it right here and now?!?*), and when, at some point, it occurred to me that I would actually need to *look* at my newly gruesome face in the mirror, panic set in.

It was then that I realized what a glorious thing initial *shock* can be. How amazing that the mind can switch off emotions and feelings and focus on information. It's the kind of shock that rushes young children past fret and toward the phone to call 911 when their parents get hurt, that allows otherwise blood-queasy people to step in and help an accident victim, that gets funerals planned in those first waves after a death.

And, as I'd discover, it's the kind of thing that allows a woman to sit in her pastor's office and claim she no longer believes in God—or at least in a God who would leave her wandering a financial desert for so long—to not only survive that but to come out with a stronger faith than ever.

In 2012, I chose *increase*—as in "increase my faith" and, I admit, "increase my bank account"—for my word of the year. Well, I'm not exactly sure I chose it as much as it was chosen *for* me and sort of smeared across my brain. Because while I had resisted jumping on this word-for-the-year bandwagon (again), I couldn't. I knew *increase* was something I needed in my life. So I claimed it, wrote about it and went public with my desire to have God increase my faith. (I kept the bank-account part private.)

The first two months were golden and wondrous; everywhere I looked, there was God doing or being something amazing. Even if we were now dependent on gifts from relatives to stay even close to financially afloat and even if a promising job prospect fell through for my husband, I believed. I trusted. I saw, felt, heard, smelled, tasted God everywhere. Until, suddenly, I couldn't. Until God and all his smells and sightings seemed to evaporate right out of my life, which went a bit dark with his absence.

Where anxiety had never been part of my life, I now spent time every day trying to still myself, trying to get my heart rate down. While I'd always pooh-poohed any ideas of "spiritual warfare," I now wore a big clunky cross under my clothes so I could feel its cool metal against my skin. I would find myself whispering Jesus' name, desperate for him to draw near, to ward off these panicky demons that seemed to dance around my heart, throwing daggers of doubt about my prayer life.

After a season of sticking to the "why" prayers and loving getting to explore the potential answers—getting to know God, what I thought was better—I ventured back into *real* prayers. After all, exploring God is all well and good, but so is eating and keeping a roof over my family's head. So as our financial crisis moved from bad to dire, my prayers became more specific. *Send a job already! Send me work! Kill some distant, ancient relative for whom I'm the secret heir! Anything, just help! Help! Help!*

And this time, as each prayer was met with nothing—no new job, no more work, no dead relative—I'd decided there could only be two options: (1) God didn't care, or (2) God wasn't there. I had grown weak and weary believing God was having us wait for some "purpose," that God was just waiting to answer prayers for the "right time." My soul got rope burns from holding on so tight to the belief that this was God doing work in us. So those devil daggers started doing their work, and I began believing, "This is all ridiculous. There is no God."

Then in mid-April, after a three-hour, solitary car ride—during which God's absence pressed hard, left me gasping for the Breath I missed—I did something I'd never done before in my life: made an appointment with a pastor, to share something I was too terrified to admit to anyone else. On the day of the appointment, I dropped into Pastor Gregg's guest chair, slunked down a bit and said, "I just don't think I believe in God anymore."

This was, of course, a big problem, I explained. Not so much because I would rot in hell (after all, our faith tradition contends that you cannot *lose* your salvation, so either way, I was "safe") but because I was under contract to write a book (this one) about finding, feeling and sensing God and his goodness all over the place. But lately, God didn't seem anywhere. He didn't even seem real.

Which I told my pastor.

Pastor Gregg's reaction to my denial of God is still one of my favorite moments of all time. When I told him I didn't believe in God, his face registered nothing. No surprise. No concern. No outrage. No smile at my silliness. Maybe because he's aware that I've been known a time *or two* to say (or write) things just for the joy of watching eyes bulge or jaws slacken, or maybe because he recognized my words as "lies from the Deceiver," as my charismatic friend later said. But as I disavowed God in my pastor's chair, he simply listened and nodded. Then he offered some *other* things I could believe about God. If I wanted.

At the end of it all, after I agreed to pray with him, Pastor Gregg suggested that I was suffering "spiritual shock." As my brain dialed back to my time of crashing faces with that horse, these words proved truer than anything else I could've heard. As I considered my spiritual injuries in the form of "unanswered prayers" and feeling abandoned or unheard, and as I considered that I believed God had inflicted these injuries, this shock made so much sense. The hurt had been so great, the prayers "ignored" for so long, the distance from God so far, that I had gone numb toward God. I couldn't feel him or see him or sense him in any way.

That was true. But, in *shock,* I could be open to God in another way.

Two weeks later, I read the scene in the novel *Glittering Images* when Father Jon Darrow, a spiritual director, declares his troubled ward also in spiritual "shock." I took in a deep, sharp breath. Though Jon Darrow was fictitious, his words were Spirit-infused nevertheless. It was true. It was what I needed to understand: where I might not feel or taste or see or smell or hear God, I *could* still let my brain take over, and let my mind and my belief alone be the place that clung to God.

While I am more of a thinker than a feeler in my daily life, and though the "life of the mind" is more important to me than the "life of the body," in my spiritual life, the reverse has always been true. I like to think *about* God, but I believe in him because I've felt him and heard him and seen him and smelled him and even tasted his presence and goodness. Because of this, no matter how wise Gregg's words had been, still I wanted my time of shock to end. So I thought I'd force the issue.

A few days after my denial of God, my youngest son and I took advantage of a lovely spring day and went to Fullersburg Woods. These were the same woods where, a year-and-a-bit earlier, I had stomped around in the snow and where I'd been convinced that God could be seen, heard, tasted, smelled and felt. These were the woods where God had been so present that I was certain that he would use this place, this time to reveal himself again to me in a mighty way—and shock me out of my shock.

No such luck.

Fredrik and I hiked down the path, over the bridge, past the trees where I'd heard the birds, felt the sun, seen the tracks. And nada. I felt nothing. So we ducked back to the place where the "Taste" sign had hung, pointing the way to the old-fashioned, pump-style drinking fountain. The post still stood, but no sign. The sign that had once seem like the very extravagance of God himself, taken down. Nonexistent. Huh.

After my son pumped himself some water and I drank some too (it tasted terrible), we returned to a patch of "beach" along the Salt Creek lagoon. I dusted off a log and sat. Fredrik stepped up to the water to try and skip a flat rock into it. I took obligatory pictures of him being five and darling and boyish at the creek, and then I grabbed a stick and began to draw in the muddy sand.

Inside, I wondered what had gone so wrong and worried that I would, indeed, lose my faith. I'd become one of those who finally succumb to the illogicality of what we profess. As I doodled in the sand, I asked God once more to make himself known. To reveal himself to me in this place.

Nothing.

Then my son stepped over my doodles and sat on the log next to me. He took a deep breath and exhaled slowly.

"It's pretty here, isn't it?" I asked him.

"Yes." He sighed again. "And quiet."

I started to talk about the quietness and all we could hear it in—the chirping, the splashing, the clomping of feet on the path behind us. Fredrik interrupted my nature lecture.

"Mama," he said, putting his hand on my leg. "Let's just be still."

Be still. The words whispered again. This time not from my never-still boy urging *me* to be still. Not even from the Spirit whose whispers I had longed for, hoped for. Instead, the words drifted as though they rose up from the splashes of the creek and then echoed deep in my mind. I closed my eyes and let the words I had memorized so many times—first as a child, then with my own kids—form fully: *Be still, and know that I am God* (Psalm 46:10).

I still *felt* nothing. No sudden rush of God's arms enveloping me. No burst of warmth from the sun or cool from the breeze. Not a heavy presence or a light lift. Of course, that's not what this verse says. God doesn't say—at least not here—to be still and *feel* or *sense* that he is God. But to know. To think. To believe. In our minds.

And I understood.

While no doubt (at least to me now) there was a bit of "spiritual warfare" happening in my soul as I sought to increase my faith—the one thing the devil would like to see diminish—God was allowing this for good. Maybe even choosing to step back from me on purpose. Because if my faith were to deepen, were to *increase,* I had to *know* that God is God even when it doesn't *feel* right. Even when I don't *feel* him. Even when I am pretty sure all of this is absurd. Even when I am at my most financially vulnerable. Especially then.

So the next spring, as the water in my basement tipped over sofas and carried bass drums across the room, I let the shock do its work—let it lead me as I woke up my husband, as I called our insurance agent and then the "catastrophe" claims folks, and as I later called the HVAC company and got an appointment to fix the furnace that had already died. And when the shock had worn off the next day and I sat crying at the kitchen table, and as the temperatures dipped below freezing and *snow* fell where the rain had been, and as I finally *felt* the weight of going through all this again and all the work that lay ahead, it was the shock—the very deadening of my senses the day before—that let me believe the conversation I once again had with God: *Who's got this, Caryn? You do, God.* And he did.

At age six, my daughter refused to believe in the Trinity. No matter how many apple or water or beaming-sunshine analogies you offered her, she stood firm in her denial. "It just makes no *sense*," she would say. And she was right. Indeed, it makes no sense. Faith is an act of the mind, not of the heart, not of the soul. Faith, really, is a response of our intellect—not our senses. Jesus tells us this.

Consider poor "doubting" Thomas, who refused to believe Jesus had risen unless he saw and touched the scars. While Thomas declared Jesus as God himself after accepting Jesus' invitation to reach out and touch him, Jesus said this: "Because you have seen me, you have believed; blessed are those who have not seen and yet have believed" (John 20:29).

While I had long taken this verse as a pat on the back from God for the faith those of us who have never seen Jesus yet still believe, sitting at the creek that day, I realized differently. Of course, I've never run my fingers across Jesus' side. I've never held his hand in mine, tracing the outline of his scars. But my faith has always been a sensory—even sensuous—one. I believe because of what I feel, of what I've smelled, tasted, seen and heard, whether in the moment or in looking back. So when the times come where I cannot or do not sense God in a way I'm used to, my faith falters. If my faith is dependent on my senses, it is hardly faith at all. Or, at least, it's not a very blessed one. According to Jesus.

In Hebrews 11:1, Jesus' definition of faith gets reworded: "Now faith is confidence in what we hope for and assurance about what we do not see" (NIV). The next verse tells us this was the kind of faith the "ancients were commended for." That's the kind of faith I want, that I long for, that only the mind—without being able to sense much at all—can give us.

And so in these moments when God seems removed, feels distant or nonexistent, when we cry out to have our deepest or most primal needs met and are kept waiting, we stand at a fork in the road. One path veers toward the belief that God not only exists and is present but that he is *good* and faithful, that Jesus saves, that the Holy Spirit emboldens—and that the earth is the Lord's and everything in it, and that it all ripples with God's presence, whether we see or feel or smell it or not. The other path veers toward a world without God, where trees bend and sway in the wind just because, and our lives are just so. It's a choice we make—to believe God *is* faithful and real and good even when he *seems* not to be—only in our minds.

Henri Nouwen says, "A waiting person is a patient person. Patience implies the willingness to stay where we are and live the situation out to the full in the belief that something hidden there will manifest itself to us."[2] Until then, we choose to believe—in our minds—that God is present and God is good.

8

Serendipity

⟨

After being still and knowing—or trying to, at least—long enough to get bored of the sand and the frogs and the sticks floating downstream, my son and I straightened our legs off the log and turned back on the path that led back to our car. Once again, we crossed the bridge and passed the banks where God had been so clear and mighty the year before. We walked past the post where a sign from God once hung. And as our feet crunched and slid on the gravel, Fredrik pointed out the "hugging tree" where his preschool class had stood for a picture. We stopped, smiled at and patted the tree—one of the oldest in these woods—and I asked if Fredrik wanted another picture. Of us hugging it this time. He shook his head no, and we pressed on toward the "welcome lodge."

Fredrik spotted the stone steps that led down from the lodge toward the stone veranda along the creek's shores. From the 1930s until the 1970s, canoes and other small vessels launched from here. Photos inside the lodge show families picnicking, umbrellas up, boats in water. But the high pollution levels of the 1970s (I still remember my teachers lamenting this in grade school) ended all that. While some still kayak and canoe in Salt Creek, this launch remains inactive. Now it's a spot for some to fish (as one older couple did that day) and at least one boy to run and explore, while his mama wandered behind.

As Fredrik tugged at the heavy, wooden doors to the lodge's basement, I ran my hands along the stone foundation walls. When one window shutter proved unlocked and loose, we peeked in, hoping to find ancient paddleboats and oars, rotting picnic tables and benches. Instead, we peered in at a room filled with stacked conference-room chairs. We laughed about our find and pressed on. While holding Fredrik's hand as he climbed up and along the stone walls, I wondered aloud what made the place so magical.

"It's magic here?" Fredrik asked.

"Not really. Just feels special, I mean."

"Like Door County."

"Good call," I said, as Fredrik grabbed my hand tighter and jumped off the wall so we could watch the fishing couple catch, wrangle and release a frog from their line.

And it was a good call. That was exactly why, I realized, this stone building in this bit of woods along a river-like creek in the near-west suburbs of Chicago dazzled me every time I was here. It *was* like Door County, Wisconsin. Specifically, like the wood-and-stone cottages and the stone walls that wound along roads in Door County's Peninsula State Park, my favorite place on earth.

I slapped my hands on my thighs, "Ready to go, bud?"

"Nope."

Instead, my son pulled me back up the stone steps, round the bend and into the lodge to see the Wooly Mammoth skeleton once more. As he walked around the display, pointing at bones, asking which they were, I noticed something remarkable. Next to the skeleton was another, glass-encased display I had looked at a billion times—with pictures of those early canoeists and picnickers, of smiling men in striped bathing suits and women with parasols.

But this time, I read what I had not read before. This lodge, the veranda and the walls my son had just climbed on and jumped from had been built by Franklin Delano Roosevelt's Depression-era Civilian Conservation Corps. As I read on, my mind tunneled a bit, zipped back to the previous summer, when I had read these same words, this same statement on a little roadside plaque in Peninsula State Park, the very one we'd just been talking about. This lodge, those lodges; this wall, those walls; these favorite places—300 miles apart—had been crafted during the same time, from the same government program, from the same types of men, desperate for work during a desperate time. Out of financial calamity had sprung two of my favorite places on earth. It was as though God wanted to remind me what he could do with hard times.

And now new words came into my mind—not words from the Psalms, as they had when we sat by the creek, but from the novel, *Cutting for Stone* by Abraham Verghese, which I'd recently read: "If ecstasy meant the sudden intrusion of the sacred into the ordinary, then it had just happened to me."[1] Maybe thirty minutes after being still and choosing to *know* that God is God, he intruded. And it was ecstasy, which I've known to be those brief moments when I'm so aware of God's hand, so keen on his message, so moved or at ease or fired up in his presence that the world blurs away, and my mind and soul zero on in on the very face of Jesus. A sort of tunnel experience—me at one end, God at the other and light in between—and we zip together, ever closer. Until, that is, life snaps me back. As was the case here, when my son—who had moved on from the mammoth fossils—wanted company as he climbed the tight-winding steps to perch in a giant bird's nest.

But the thing I love so much about Verghese's definition of ecstasy is that, though it's not the definition *Merriam-Webster's*

Dictionary or anywhere else seems to give, it's spot on for what I've known to be true in my life. It's pitch perfect for the ways, sometimes, God appears and takes my breath away, leaves me reeling just before releasing me back into the realities of life.

And for me—as for Marion Stone, the character who pronounces this about ecstasy in *Cutting for Stone*—often these ecstasies are not induced by any super-spiritual quest or even from extended times of stillness or silence. Instead, they are serendipitous.

I had no idea what *serendipity* meant, but when I saw it spelled out on the cover of a book and worked out its pronunciation, I knew I needed to know. I walked away from the book carousel repeating the word again and again, letting its syllables slither off my tongue and then pop from my lips: *ser-en-dip-i-ty, serendipity, serendipity.* I didn't want to forget it by the time I found my mom and could ask what it meant.

Serendipity, my mom told me, is like a happy accident, a wonderful coincidence. I loved the idea of this immediately and have loved the idea ever since. Of course, serendipity melds wonderfully with my love of the mysterious, my belief that good things come from exploration. And indeed they do. Some of the most important discoveries and medical cures have come serendipitously.

According to the promotional copy for the book *Happy Accidents,* "penicillin, chemotherapy drugs, X-rays, Valium, the Pap smear, and Viagra were all discovered accidentally, stumbled upon in search of something else."[2]

And it's in this searching for something else that we often stumble into God's presence, stumble right onto holy ground. Certainly it's how many have "found" Jesus. I think of the Magi, following a star in search of a prince born high in a palace, stumbling onto Jesus toddling around a carpenter's workshop. I think of the woman at the well, searching for some fresh water, stumbling into the Messiah and his "living water." I think of Mary heading to the tomb that Sunday morning, searching for a way to properly bury Jesus, stumbling into her risen Lord. And I think today of all those searching for peace or love or comfort in hit after hit of something, only to stumble into their Comforter in a random conversation, in a line from a novel or in the encouragement of a twelve-step program.

Certainly this has been true for me: in my searches for something else entirely—sometimes simply searching for information, sometimes an escape, sometimes that peace or love or comfort— I have stumbled, happy-accidentally into Jesus. It's what happened that day, reading those words in the lodge. Where I had longed, just minutes before, for some *feeling* to sweep through me, God used serendipity to make himself known.

And it wasn't simply because of the *coincidence* that my two favorite places were built at the same time and by the same organization. It was because of the *time* and the *manner* in which they were built that made it especially Jesus-y, that made me smile and roll my eyes up at God, whom once again I sensed smirking at me.

The first—and the smirkiest—was simply that this place I loved so was built by Big Government. Here's the deal: I had just written two back-to-back articles professing my libertarian leanings. And now this. (Shoot, maybe my friends are right. Maybe God really *is* a socialist!)

The second—and the least smirky, actually—was that, as I sat by the creek with my boy, trying to be still and know, I had been nearly ready to step away from God because he had gone silent, because my family was in such dire need of financial rescue, and because I was tired of following a God who'd let us wander for so long. I was tired of the hurt, worn down by this dark time of life.

And here I was reading that my favorite places were born out of the *Great Depression*—out of one of the darkest, most difficult times in our nation's history. While I'd never claim that God orchestrated a global economic downturn so that, one day, I could see the delight that rose from despair, certainly God did use it to remind me in that moment. Remind me that he is sovereign, that he is at work and that he makes good.

All this from a chance encounter, from the random. Happy accident, indeed.

I realize, of course, serendipities and these sorts of everyday ecstasies are easily written off, shrugged away. Certain types claim this drains theology or God of his bigness, of his power, of his universal focus by making it all about me and my little moments with Jesus. As if God's got nothing better to do than to orchestrate a little, happy accident for me. Such a First World, egocentric God encounter, some would say.

And other types just don't buy into coincidences or serendipities at all. Happenstance is happenstance, certainly not holy. Consider this:

> For those with a highly empirical bent, a coincidence is happenstance, a simultaneous collision of two events that has no special significance and obeys the laws of probability. "In reality, the most astonishingly incredible coincidence imaginable would be the complete absence of all coinci-

dence," says John Allen Paulos, professor of mathematics at
Temple University in Philadelphia, and best-selling author
of *Innumeracy: Mathematical Illiteracy and Its Consequences.*
"Believing in the significance of oddities is self-aggrandizing,"
he adds. "It says, 'Look how important I am.'"[3]

Indeed. It's this sense of self-importance or center-of-the-
universe-ness that keeps certain science-y sorts from embracing
the significance of serendipity, but it's also what keeps certain
Christian sorts from it too.

And I get that. Except, well, I didn't make up that I'm important to God. We're not being egotistical if we believe God
swoops in just for us every now and again. We're not the ones
who declared ourselves the "apple of God's eye" (Deuteronomy
32:10; Psalm 17:8; Zechariah 2:8). God's Word says that. Several
times. And I like to believe it. I like to believe that God not only
sees me but keeps me front and center, looking at me through
his perfect lenses. What makes this *not* particularly egocentric is
my belief that it's not *just* me in the bull's-eye of God's focus. God
keeps me and her and that guy over there and all of creation
front and center—as only God can do.

But God's Word has more to say about this, about serendipity,
that is. And I find I can't dismiss serendipity as insignificant or
self-centered, because that would mean I'd have to dismiss so
much of the Bible as mere happenstance. It would mean that we
read through the genealogy of Jesus and just go, "Huh. What are
the chances that *the* Messiah would descend from these folks whose
stories fill the Old Testament? What are the chances that Rahab
would become Ruth's great-great-whatever grandmother?" Was it
God, or was it coincidence? Was it some sort of sacred serendipity,
or was it that everyone had amazing stories like this and that David's family tree was so huge that everybody was related to Jesus?

Dismissing serendipity as a means of detecting God's presence and goodness would mean that I would have to assume that the Bible is not the story of God's hand at work through his people but that it was a back-peddled or forced fabrication. Dismissing serendipity as an instrument of grace would mean reading through a story like (Dream Coat) Joseph's with a shrug and a yawn. *Whatever. Guy got lucky. Finally caught some good karma.* It would be a story of nothing more than bad breaks (the being-tossed-into-a-pit-and-then-sold-into-slavery-by-his-brothers *and* the being-falsely-accused-and-tossed-in-the-slammer things) and good ones (like that being-able-to-interpret-dreams-and-having-Pharaoh-catch-wind-of-that-skill thing). It would be nothing more than a probabilities equation that Joseph was the guy his brothers needed to see about some grain. It'd be nothing more than one stroke of dumb (good or bad) luck after another. And what would be the point? At least, I mean, the point of it being in the Bible?

Whether it's in reading the Scriptures or living in this world, if all we can ask is, "Huh? What are the chances?" then we deny God—at least, we deny a God at work, a God who is able, a God who is present, a God who suddenly intrudes into our everyday, lets the rest of the world disappear around us, and sucks us right into his holy presence. Just because he loves us. Just because we are the apples of his eye. Just because sometimes when we're scraping along, God wants us to find him and to find him good.

Imaginary

For my fortieth birthday, my eight-year-old daughter—an artist since she emerged from the womb—handed me a gift bag stapled shut and stuffed with hand-glittered, crumpled-up tissue paper. As I dug through handfuls of tissue, I finally discovered the gift at the bottom. I unwrapped more tissue as she pronounced the gift: a "wish candle."

Greta had recently discovered the fine duct-tape arts. She'd crafted cell phones and mirrors, wallets and frames, all sorts of jewelry and accessories for her dolls—all out of duct tape. But this wish candle was something new to me. Greta twirled two strands of duct tape into a candle shape and secured two pennies at the top. This way, I could "see a penny, pick it up and all the day have good luck," and I got not one but two—in candle form so that I could blow them out and make a wish. Good luck *and* a wish. Whenever I wanted.

I'm not being dramatic when I say that I'm not sure I could've gotten a better gift for my fortieth birthday. That was the birthday—the decade—I'd been looking forward to for a good, long year. Amid the many blessings the thirties had brought me (my kids not least among them), my thirties proved difficult, to say the least. It was a decade spent trying to figure out life as it unraveled and U-turned and took off in new, often-unwanted directions.

But as I've come to understand (think different!), perhaps this was what that decade was *supposed to be* for me. God used my thirties—the good, bad and ugly of it—to work me over into who and where I was supposed to be, and I'd gotten the sense that my forties would be where it could all start coming together. So I approached forty not with fear or worry about aging and getting old but with wonder and excitement. I anticipated forty as I had sixteen: with a sense that *this* was when life was really going to get good. And I haven't been much disappointed.

Turns out, this optimism thing really *does* work. Instead of wondering what shoe was going to drop next, I began to imagine what God had in store, began to dream about the various longings of my heart and how God would meet them. In short, my praying became less about demands or calls for rescue but more like wishes. Although the word *wish* might not get much play in Christian circles, God takes them pretty seriously. At least, according to Saint Paul and King David.

First consider Paul's toast to God: "Now to him who is able to do immeasurably more than all we ask or imagine, according to his power that is at work within us, to him be glory in the church and in Christ Jesus throughout all generations, for ever and ever! Amen" (Ephesians 3:20).

Hear, hear!

Then consider David's lovely command: "Take delight in the LORD and he will give you the desires of your heart" (Psalm 37:4).

Seems to me that if we love God and seek his will, God is interested in what we imagine and in what we desire. He is interested in what we wish for. And he's a God who takes our wishes and does one better. He surpasses what we can dream up.

Beyond that, God not only grants the desires in our hearts, he places those desires there in the first place.

So when we wish, when we dream, when we imagine, he's there with us, in that place. When I wished for and imagined my family out of our financial pit and living once again financially free—giving, traveling, going to the grocery store without stress!—God was there, listening, orchestrating, preparing, smiling for the time when those wishes "come true" in *some* form or another. Not because he's a genie and we've rubbed his bottle the right way, but because he is good and he is with us— especially when we imagine him so.

Katie was so earnest when she said it. Her eyes fixed, her eyebrows drawn together, her lips pulled straight. "Just imagine *Jesus* is sitting there," Katie said. "In a rocking chair or something. That keeps you out of trouble."

This was Katie's advice—as told to her by her parents—on how to manage our teenage years without going "too far" with boys, or without giving in to the temptations of beer or pot or cigarettes or whatever else lingered. All we had to do was *imagine* Jesus sitting there.

I asked Katie why that made a difference, why Jesus needed to be in a rocking chair in the corner.

Katie went on and on about how, when we picture Jesus there, it's like we've gotten "caught" before we've done anything. It's worse than having a mom or dad there, because Jesus would see us and would know *forever* what we had done. This, she said, was the best advice she had ever gotten. This, she said, was the thing that kept her from messing up. And messing around, I supposed.

I immediately realized the problem for me. I had—since that first day when I realized God heard and saw me—imagined Jesus with me all the time. But it didn't keep me from a whole lot of sin. I mean, at fourteen my sins weren't all that bad, but I had a pretty active imagination when it came to Jesus being around, in all areas of my life. And the idea that Jesus was there—even if I hadn't yet pictured him rocking in a corner, every now and again lifting his eyes from his knitting to see what evil I was up to—hadn't kept me from gossiping or lying to a friend or talking back to my mother.

Years later, when I was in college and deep into my rebellion from God "phase," I remembered Katie's advice and proved my fourteen-year-old self right. One night, I conjured up that image of Rocking Chair, Knitting, Peering-Over-His-Reading-Glasses Jesus and wondered if it could stop me from my sins. It didn't. Once again, just because I *knew* Jesus was there, seeing and knowing, I didn't care. That's what rebellion is, right? Flagrant disobedience. Choosing wrong—smack dab in the face of what's right.

But it's been nearly thirty years since I first heard this piece of advice, and I've never been able to shake it. I still believe the way Katie presented it to be foolish, not to mention wrongheaded. I don't think it does much good to imagine any sort of Gotcha Jesus lurking about, waiting for us to screw up. I don't believe for one second that the Jesus who was beaten, whipped and nailed to a cross for our sins—before we ever committed them—crouches in any corner ready to spring up and point.

"Aha!" Jesus does not say. "Got you again, sucka!"

But imagining Jesus, God and the Holy Spirit with me, imagining specific attributes and situations, imagining facial expressions, or imagining their presence has proved to be a gift in my life. It's been something that has at times convicted, at times comforted, at times counseled. Imagining God has encouraged me, strengthened me and equipped me. But it matters that we imagine God *correctly*. Not that each of us will imagine him the same, but I hope our images are God-breathed—not shame-induced, as my friend Katie's were.

I've often wondered: had my friend encouraged me to imagine Jesus, slouched in a love seat, his arm slung up against the back, with a big empty space for me next to him, sighing or maybe strumming his index finger against the round, red scar on his hand, would that have made a difference? Would that image— rather than one of Jesus rocking and knitting and scolding— kept me from various "big" sins in my life? After all, rebelling against one who loves us enough to forgive and make space for us—no matter what—is a lot harder than rebelling against a persnickety, nosey taskmaster.

It's hard to know. Impossible. Besides, rebellion is a heart issue. And if my heart wasn't in the right place, it didn't matter what or who I saw. And yet, who and what I see, what I picture and imagine as I go about my daily life, makes all the difference for the issues in my heart.

Consider: if folks could see *me* most mornings in the shower (and be sure, I'm very glad they cannot!), they'd see my mouth moving as I talk to my muse. I've long said two things about her: one, her name is Chaos, for she appears usually in the midst of screaming and clambering kids, and she beckons me back into the dark corners of my mind for a little chat. That said (and this would be two), she lives in my bathroom. Mostly because, although she appears and beckons me in the midst of chaos, she speaks most clearly in peace. And, as is famously the case for mothers of young kids, the bathroom is often the only peaceful place.

So, for years, Chaos and I have conversed while I scratch shampoo deep into my scalp. We've explored ideas while I

finger-comb in conditioner; we've asked hard questions while
I've lathered up the bar of soap; we've laughed at first remem-
brances of hilarious stories (*How could we have forgotten that?!?!*)
while I ran a razor up my legs.

I talk to Chaos and she talks to me. Sure, it's in my own voice
with words rolling off my own tongue, but it's Chaos talking.
This little tête-à-tête between Chaos and me is as integral a part
of my writing process as sitting down to type. I often rush out
of the bathroom, towel still on my head, blinking my contacts
into place, to jot down some of our conversations.

But, for all the years Chaos and I have chatted, I've also realized something else: of course, Chaos isn't really my muse;
she's the Holy Ghost. Which means all this time I've really been
talking to God and believing God talks to me. About writing.
About stories. About life. In the shower.

For years, my shower-time conversations with God, believing
God really spoke through his Spirit, through my mouth, were
something I'd never think to share with anyone. My fellow
artists can barely handle that I make up my own muse (Chaos
is not, in fact, one of the nine daughters of Zeus and Mne-
mosyne[1]). So I figured the rest of it would be a bit much for
most people.

But then Jonalyn Fincher wrote a piece that astounded me. "I
take long walks in our White Woods among the aspen," Fincher
writes. "I ask God about what's troubling me. I've had long conversations about my family, my mistakes or what I'm supposed
to speak on next. I try to answer myself with an open spirit to
what God might be saying. I write down what I think I hear him
saying and then compare it with Scripture."[2]

Here was someone I knew and respected, someone who's a
Christian apologist by trade, and as devout and orthodox a
follower of Jesus as I know—admitting that she walks and talks

with and *for* God. She got the idea from Frank Laubach who himself writes, "I have just returned from a walk alone, a walk so wonderful that I feel like reducing it to a universal rule, that all people ought to take a walk every evening all alone where they can talk aloud without being heard by anyone, and that during this entire walk they all ought to talk with God, allowing Him to use their tongue to talk back—and letting God do most of the talking."[3]

While this practice may startle some, in fact this brings me into God's presence in a more focused way than the "regular," silent, one-way prayer. Of course, to have a conversation like this with God—to believe that God himself uses our own mouths to speak his truth—requires a lot of Scripture-reading (as God rolls Scripture-esque words over my tongue more often than not), a lot of focused and repetitive "warm-up" prayer (I like the Lord's Prayer to get me in the zone), and a good bit of imagination.

After all, when we have conversations with God, a la Fincher and Laubach, we are imagining God is right there with us, walking alongside us in those woods, sitting in the passenger seat as we drive, maybe brushing his almighty teeth in the sink next to us while we shower. To converse with God means we imagine him there. He *is* there, of course, but we imagine him, not in the spiritual realm but in the physical. And that takes a bit of pretending to pull off.

"To know God intimately," writes Tanya Marie Luhrmann, a professor of anthropology at Stanford University, "you need to use your imagination, because the imagination is the means humans must use to know the immaterial."[4]

So true. Though, as Luhrmann clarifies, this doesn't mean that God is made up, that God is just for pretend. But it is only through our imaginations—this wonderful, creative gift from God himself—that we can conceive of God at all. We weren't there to see Jesus in person. We cannot quantify or prove when we "feel" the Spirit move. What becomes holy ground still appears as regular ground to others. Where we see the kingdom of God, others see this same creaky world. It's our imagination of God that makes the difference here.

And God encourages us to use our imaginations to know him. We have a faith built on it, really. To read the Bible *well* requires putting our imagination caps on. To bring ourselves into the grand story of God and his people means we must imagine what we don't know for sure, what we cannot see, what we cannot smell, hear, feel or taste. To know God, to live with him and to live aware of his presence means learning what we can for sure and then letting the rest *become* as it swirls around in our minds.

Again, God is helpful here. In his Word, God invites us to imagine him as everything from the sustaining Bread of Life to the rescuing Rock, from the comforting God With Us to the lofty King of Kings, from the all-encompassing I Am to the head-scratching Word, from the Abba Father to the Mother Hen, God gives us images to *imagine* him, to see with our minds what we cannot with our eyes. With these words, God invites us to find holy ground in our pretend.

When I was a sports- and board-game-hating kid, *play* was synonymous with *pretend*. My best friend and I played "office," "school," "store" or "library." We imagined we were corporate executives and spent hours setting up our desks, arranging pens in pen holders and restacking our legal pads. We hauled out our play chalkboards and took turns being the teacher, reading aloud from the thick, spiral-bound teacher's manuals my teacher-godmother gave me. We made scanners out of red, plastic-tipped bottle-openers, as we scanned and "beeped" the books that make-believe patrons would check out. We set up an orange-buttoned adding machine on a long table, stacked folded brown bags at the end and crafted grocery-store checkout lines. Bagging those groceries was our earliest form of Tetris.

When I grew up—and performed variations of the jobs I'd once pretended to do—something struck me. What we'd imagined wasn't that far off. Just because we made believe and made *up* didn't make it untrue. Volunteering at my son's middle-school library was very much as we'd pretended (though the scanner was even cooler). The way I interacted with customers while working at a children's clothing store one summer during college turned out to be just like the way I'd interacted with imaginary customers during grade-school summers. The real-life first-graders I read to piped up more than the pretend ones, but sitting cross-legged on a stool, in front of a roomful of students, reading from a book my godmother had given me turned out to feel much like I'd imagined.

The same can be said for the hours I pretended to be a writer while playing alone in my room. In fact, I wrote my first actual book while sitting at the off-white, gold-trimmed corner desk that I wrote limericks at as a girl. I've conducted real-life radio interviews while perched on my daughter's bed, the same one I'd used as a girl to pretend I was being interviewed—when the removable tips of the bed's four posters had been microphones while the end of the bed became the chairs for the Phil Donahue show. Now, while I've never been interviewed in my bedroom by Phil Donahue, my imaginings of what it was *like* to be asked about a project, about what's new or what's next were pretty right on.

One of the problems people have about using the word *imag-*

ination for our faith, as a way to experience the presence of God, is that we assume that what we imagine cannot be real, cannot be true. But this is wrong. Pure and simple. Just because we imagine something, just because we pretend, does not mean it isn't real or that it doesn't exist or that it isn't true.

Think of what we'd have missed in life if scientists and explorers and artists and mathematicians and mystics never imagined that there was more than what we see. Imagining trips to the moon made it possible. Imagining that the earth was round was eventually proved correct. Imagining a country where all people were created equal sparked a revolution to make it so (or closer to so).

What we imagine often determines what is real in our lives— at least when it's tied to what we *desire.* The games I played as a child reflected my real desires. I wanted to do those things, hoped that having a tidy desk with stacks of notepads and vials of pens, that being surrounded by books, able to push buttons and smile at people, would in some way be part of my future. So once upon a time I pretended they were—and today, much of it has "come true" in some capacity.

What we imagine reflects what we desire; our pretend reflects our longings for a real thing. Even imaginary monsters under the bed and a call to Mom or Dad can reflect a real desire to see danger rooted out, to be made safe, to have our fears taken away.

And so it is when we imagine God, when we pretend he is there, walking with us, talking with us, brushing his teeth while we shave our legs, patting the cushion on the loveseat for us. We imagine God when we desire him to be with us—and just because we're imagining him doesn't make it wrong.

Last summer—on the first coolish, crispish summer morning after a week of scorching 100-degree days—I took my Bible and copy of *Jesus Calling* out to my back deck. I laughed when I noticed the steam rising up from my cup of coffee. The nice, Christian lady out doing her "quiet time" on the back deck as the sun rose (albeit, on the *other* side of the house): such a stereotype. But one I'd certainly never nailed before.

If Chaos is my muse and my muse is really the Holy Spirit, it makes sense that God and I often find each other and speak to each other best as I retreat into my mind in the middle of noise. Though silence and solitude are tried and true spiritual practices, I fail at them constantly. Mostly because, in silence and calm and peace and quiet, my soul and mind get restless. And true to form, as I sat like the Good Christian Lady on my back deck with my steaming coffee, almost right away I noticed the "teenage" bunny and mentally remarked how big he'd gotten. I wondered if I could go cut the tops off some strawberries. *If I toss some into that weed patch, will he find them? Will he eat them? Or will my human scent drive him away?*

And then the neighbor's car beeped twice. Doors unlocked, an alarm shut off from the remote. Huh? The neighbor normally doesn't leave for work this early. But then I noticed their son— the *human* teenager. *Ah, yes. Up for baseball. Makes sense.*

And while God is indeed the God of all these things, my mind had not exactly stayed focused on him. Hence my trouble with "quiet time" and this particular discipline.

So I kicked back in my deck chair and looked across the potted mint plants to the white loveseat against the deck rail. The image started fuzzy but sharpened as the coffee kicked in. I imagined Jesus sitting there—cross-legged, adjusting the ever-slipping red cushions. He had khaki shorts on—a bit ragged around the edges—and a tan *ThinkChristian* T-shirt. I got mine because I'm a regular contributor to the site, but I wondered how he got his. Didn't matter—what an endorsement! Jesus wearing your T-shirt? *I'll have to tell Josh* (the editor), I thought.

Already, my focus on Jesus was slipping, so I just started talking.

"So Jesus," I said, "you really are more present in these early, backyard quiet times I'm always reading about."

I smiled. He smiled back.

"Not more," Jesus said, through my mouth. "Just always."

I sighed, pulling a face. Might as well get truthful, to the point here. I never know when a child will wake and come yelling for me.

"I'm getting a little tired of the waiting, you know."

"I know."

"Can you give me a clue? A little hint as to how much longer?"

"Soon," he said.

"And very soon?" I smile again. Jesus laughed. He knows how I love the old spirituals.

"But Jesus, really? We're getting kind of desperate here. We've taken huge steps and big leaps of faith—in obedience. We're trying to follow you, and you're still sort of leaving us hanging."

"Not hanging. You just don't see."

"Right," I said. "You know the plans you have for us, yada, yada, yada."

"Yes," he says. "And they are not plans to harm you. As you know."

"It sure doesn't feel that way. It feels like you brought us into this desert to die."

"No. I go ahead of you," Jesus said, "I'm knocking down mountains and leveling roads for you. This desert is going to blossom. Remember, I've called you by name. You are mine. I've got you."

I sighed and turned to watch the bunny who had hopped back into the patch of clover beyond the patio. "Right," I said. "And in the meantime, I suppose, you'll say that when I pass through the waters, you will be with me; when I pass through the rivers, they won't sweep over me. When I walk through these fires, I won't get burned; the flames won't get me. For you are God, the Holy One, my Savior [see Isaiah 43:2-3]. And you've got me."

I sensed that Jesus was smiling again. (He knows this is one of only a few passages I know by heart.) But when I turned back, Jesus was gone. Well, my image of him at least.

The whole thing was only in my imagination. But it was true and real. And God was present in the pretend.

The week after I sat on my deck, I'd celebrate my fortieth birthday. Forty, the year I'd imagined everything finally turning around. That day, my fortieth birthday, my husband would get a job offer. One month later, I'd receive my own job offer and then sign a contract for another book.

Neither job—nor any book contract—wiped away all of our worry or erased all our debt. Together, they barely paid our bills. In meeting this need, God didn't remove our lovely dependence on him. But in this, God showed he is as we imagine him—when we imagine finding him with us and finding him good.

10

Dazzled

〈

The memory of the morning still makes me dizzy. Of course, now I see it as a dream, but even as I lived it, I felt my body floating above, looking down—amazed.

There I sat, at a round, pine table on a paneled porch. I saw a chipmunk scurry across log-stump chairs; I heard a loon (or something) caw and scream as it flew across the plane of windows. If I stretched and bent my neck a bit, I could see the swim platform my kids rocked on and jumped from. And just moments before, the sun rose—shimmering and shimmying across the ripples of the black lake below. Though I couldn't see it clearly because the pines and birches and oaks stretched so boldly, so brashly—as they should have, as to block the sunrise and not mar one bit of the beauty of it is no small feat. Those trees should have been bold and brash and proud.

But maybe it wasn't pride they were showing, maybe it was worship. Their limbs were stretched out in praise, of "I love you *this* much" to their Creator. It's certainly how mine were right then, as all I could do was look around, smile at that scampery chipmunk again, and say: *Oh, wow. Oh, God. Oh, wow.*

Not that long ago, I'd seen pictures of this place. I'd seen the shots of my friends' kids rocking on and jumping off that very same platform. I'd seen photos of my friend writing away at this same table, overlooking this same black lake under these same worship-y trees. And my heart had burst with envy, seeping green through every last cell, fiber, sinew, bone and bit of blood in my body. While we suffered so financially, while we worried about losing our very home, this friend had enjoyed all this, I thought.

It isn't fair. It makes no sense how God can prosper some and let other falter, was all I could think at the time. I would have bet that my friend didn't even love the place as I would. She wouldn't even understand that what I was seeing in those pictures of her kids—jumping and swimming and laughing in life vests and canoes, on swim platforms and waterskis—had been what I once dreamt of for my own family. Nothing fancy. Just happy family togetherness. In the woods. By the water. Was that too much to ask from God?

So when this friend texted me, asking if my family would like to use her cabin—that very same one I had longed for those years ago—last summer, as grateful as I was to my friend, it was God I couldn't get over. Where God should've probably punished me somehow or in some way for my envy—for my discontentment with my own life and my own blessings, for questioning his goodness—God not only forgave me for that, but he saw deeper, straight through to my longings and my desires. He loved me enough to give me an otherwise unaffordable vacation for the price of gas and groceries, to give me some moments with my family as I'd only ever dreamt of.

And so, on that first night, as I watched my kids swim and jump and laugh and fight on that very same swim platform I had seen my friend's kids jumping from, and that next morning, as I watched those pines and maples and white birches continuing their stretch, as the ferns crept close to the porch and as that chipmunk dashed from chair to railroad tie to under a tiny pine, I turned my eyes toward God. And he shrugged at me, opened his hand, waved his holy arm and said, *Here. This. Now. Because I love you.*

And there, in God's presence, his goodness so thick and warm and enveloping, I could hardly breathe, let alone thank him. And yet I did—a whispery, sniffly thanks. Because wow, just wow.

In announcing her book *Help, Thanks, Wow: The Three Essential Prayers*, Anne Lamott says that the first two prayers described in the title should be familiar to her readers (as they were to me), since she's written about these two types of prayer before. But, Lamott writes, "A few years ago, I added the praise-and-amazement prayer, Wow."[1] I'm glad she did. I admit, though, that *Wow* is an easy prayer to forget when we're either lost in times of desperation or else so relieved, wrapped up in gratitude, that we fail to notice all the ways God simply *wows*, dazzles and delights his beloveds.

And God wows, dazzles and delights us all the dang time. Not just when we're breathing woods-and-water air, watching boats skim, or hearing animals (*bear? deer? raccoon?*) tramp and crackle below the windows. Not just when we can exhale a bit because we've got jobs (and dental insurance!) waiting for us when we return from vacation. Not just when the huge, un-expected, lifelong dreams are met, but in the everyday, in the routine. In both. In all. God does do "immeasurably more than all we ask or imagine" (Ephesians 3:20).

Not that the world and its glory is all about us—certainly not. Everything—and everyone—exists to praise and please God. But

God placed *us* in this world too. He set us here with eyes and
ears and noses and tastebuds and feelers to enjoy the world and
to see him in it, to be astounded by his goodness in all of life—to
join in with the world's praise and be dazzled by the glory all
around us.

Consider the words in Isaiah 55:1, 6, 9-13:

Come, all you who are thirsty,
    come to the waters;
and you who have no money,
    come, buy and eat!
Come, buy wine and milk
    without money and without cost. . . .

Seek the LORD while he may be found;
    call on him while he is near. . . .

"As the heavens are higher than the earth,
    so are my ways higher than your ways
    and my thoughts than your thoughts.
As the rain and the snow
    come down from heaven,
and do not return to it
    without watering the earth
and making it bud and flourish,
    so that it yields seed for the sower and bread for the eater,
so is my word that goes out from my mouth:
    It will not return to me empty,
but will accomplish what I desire
    and achieve the purpose for which I sent it.
You will go out in joy
    and be led forth in peace;
the mountains and hills

will burst into song before you,
and all the trees of the field
will clap their hands.
Instead of the thornbush will grow the juniper,
and instead of briers the myrtle will grow.
This will be for the Lord's renown,
for an everlasting sign,
that will endure forever."

I'm torn on what I love most about this chapter of Isaiah. The word-lover in me gets entranced by the language, the imagery, the cadence. But, of course, the God-lover in me can't stop smiling about the *invitation* this passage is to seek God in the beauty of this world: to lose ourselves in the joy of singing and clapping trees, to share in the decadent gifts of milk and wine he offers simply because he loves us, to see blue-berried junipers as both glorifying God and existing as a sign of God's love. Amazing.

Technically, water is enough to quench thirst in this world. But God dazzles with milk and wine. Technically, seeds are all that are needed for trees to reproduce. But God dazzles with buds and flourishes. And he invites us to see him in this—to let us know that he is near, that he loves us, and that he is good every time we take a sip or every time we see a blossom. God longs to be noticed, to be sought in each bit of beauty or oddness. Delving into the *glory* of God is a bit like delving into his mystery. To wonder about God's wonder is like the hidden door and secret passage straight to God's heart.

In an article about how weirded out many reporters get when it comes to people's faith and how they should report on religion like they do crimes, Sarah Pulliam Bailey writes about her reaction to reading a story about the first female Olympic boxer:

> I flipped to the story about the first female boxer right away. It combines everything, as an American woman, I'm supposed to love: The Olympics, America, women, strong women, boxing, something new, the first woman at something.
>
> So I'm reading through, grinning and all of that, and then I hit this sentence.
>
>> The headphone dangling from her left ear was playing Christian hymns. She used to listen to Drake and Eminem, but she found that rap music riled her up too much before a fight. When she gets in the ring, she wants to be calm—to think about each punch, and never just throw it.
>
> Wait, what?
>
> She listens to Christian hymns? Besides getting her calm, when, where, why, how did she start that? Is it just something from her upbringing, or is there some faith element there? If she is a Christian, does she feel any tension between her faith and boxing? Or is everything a-OK? Or maybe she isn't religious at all and just uses hymns to calm herself?
>
> I don't know. But I can't tell anything specific from that sentence.[2]

In this article, intended to encourage members of the press to approach religion reporting as they do crime reporting, Bailey hits on something we Christians ought to do all the time when it comes to God. And she sums it up in her simple, good-reporter reaction of "Wait, what?"

Without "Wait, what?" ready to jump out of your mind anytime you read or see or notice something quirky or off, I'd argue that you have no business being a reporter (or a detective among other things, I imagine). Without letting curiosity get the best of you, without catching oddities and asking follow-up questions, no journalist's story can ever be more than a recitation—even a well-crafted one—of facts. Without "Wait, what?" a story will only ever inform; it cannot compel or intrigue. "Wait, what?" turns covering routine town-hall meetings into uncovering political corruption. "Wait, what?" has brought down presidents, has convicted criminals, has cleaned up communities.

But "Wait, what?" doesn't only seek to take down. "Wait, what?" is the central question of those who desire to live dazzled and delighted, of those who want to dive deep into life and discover all its amazements. "Wait, what?" propels adventurers, sparks artists and pushes scientists. "Wait, what?" is the beginning of learning, of seeking, of trying to understand.

And "Wait, what?" should be a central question to the Christian faith—if we dig deeper into the Bible, into our faith traditions and into our understanding of God, certainly. But more than that, "Wait, what?" is essential if we want to be dazzled and delighted by God.

Because it's in this question that we notice, pause and ask, which leads us to discover the amazing things God offers us every single day. It's what causes us to stop and gawk with others at the rainbow above, but it's also what can cause us to stop and gawk at the God who created it, at what he might be giving us with that rainbow. "Wait, what?" means our minds have noticed, paused and asked, so when a friend offers us her cabin and when we end up splashing, jumping, playing and laughing in the same spot that caused such envy just a few years ago, we *wait* and ask *what* it is that God wants us to know.

The answer, which I've found time and again, is that God chooses to go over and above, chooses to astound, to overwhelm us with blessings and goodness because he loves us and because he wants us to know that this world is steeped with his presence. That we should not be able to so much as look at a juniper bush or take a sip of wine without being dazzled and delighted—because we see or taste God in it, because we know that the Creator is with us.

In his book *Living the Lord's Prayer,* Albert Haase writes of something Thomas Merton called the "rabbitness of God," and he says:

> Creatures like giraffes and turnips, in being what the Creator intended them to be, offer God glory and provide a reminder: the more a creature is what God intends it to be, the more it is a clear reflection of the Creator. . . .
>
> Each thing of creation points to the hands of its Creator and becomes a reflection of the Divine. Creation mirrors God like a Wisconsin lake reflecting the sunset.[3]

Indeed.

Though this idea was never officially spelled out for me and though the "rabbitness of God" wasn't common vernacular, this idea that God could be seen so clearly in creation was part and parcel of my faith upbringing. When I was six, my dad and I joined the YMCA's "Indian Princesses" program. It took about one session (the costume and jewelry helped) for me to become obsessed with all things Native American. I became enraged when anyone said Columbus discovered America (*How does one discover something when people are living there?*), but I also worried about the faith of these first Americans. Particularly, that of my favorite tribe, the Hopi. I worried about their worship of the sun—or Tawa, the Sun Spirit. I wanted them to worship *God*—not the sun.

But my mom—in what is sure to sound like heresy to some, but to me, was one of the first great moments in my faith—said, "When they saw the sun and worshiped it, it really was an acknowledgment of the sun's Creator." She said the same would be for someone who worshiped a rock. Or a tree. That what they marvel at isn't always—or usually—the thing itself but the power behind it. Whether or not they have the right words or theology, my mom told me, the Hopi were seeking God as he revealed himself through creation. My first lesson in general revelation.

The second way this played out was much more orthodox, but closely related. One of the benefits of growing up in the Reformed tradition is the teaching of Abraham Kuyper's "sphere sovereignty." While "old" (as quite opposed to the "neo" set) Reformed folks didn't always live this out, the general idea was that there is no distinction between sacred and secular. Kuyper's famous quote on this is: "Oh, no single piece of our mental world is to be hermetically sealed off from the rest, and there is not a square inch in the whole domain of our human existence over which Christ, who is Sovereign over *all*, does not cry: 'Mine!'"[4]

This quote gets a lot of play, yet I think its truth is still underestimated. That Jesus cries "mine" over all our ideas, over all actions, over every last bit of this world speaks to God's presence, his work, in all of it. It means that every last thing, every last thought, every last action, every last piece of earth, sky and water has God's name stamped on it, is made holy by his ownership and sovereignty.

And when we stop and notice all that dazzles and delights, and ask "Wait, what?" the answer always is: God, with us—here, now—going above and beyond to dazzle and delight us with his mercy, goodness and work in our lives. The God who, while we were yet sinners, sent his Son to die for the forgiveness of our sins, who took the burden from us, and who then sent his Holy Spirit to dwell in us, to roar passion in us and to waft cool, breezy peace within us (see Romans 5:8). This God is the God who loves us even when we don't love him, who hears us when we cannot hear him, who never leaves us even when he feels so far away. He's the God who reveals himself through all of creation—and whom all of creation cries out to. He's the God who always does more than we can imagine or hope for even. He's the God who amazes us with his goodness when we stop and notice. He's the God who's at work *now* and invites us to delight in him in this moment, to sense his presence in the present—not just by remembering what he *has* done or hoping for what he *will* do, but by being dazzled and delighted and amazed by God, the one with us in this moment, in this place. Wherever that is, we find him and we find him good.

11

Safaris

I was all ready to point it out.

"Fredrik," I said. "It's coming up."

"What?"

"The church I was baptized in. You had asked. Remember?"

"Oh. Where?"

I slowed our car and extended my arm and pointing finger. "There . . ." But then I stopped, put down my arm.

St. Luke's Lutheran Church was now my town's Masonic Temple. *Masons!* I cursed in my mind.

First they taunted me with their tantalizing, creepy secrets, their skull-and-bone-ish lairs and their mysterious markings on the dollar bills, and now they overtook my first church? While perhaps the purchase was a saving grace to St. Luke's, to me it was nothing short of shocking and scandalous.

But I pulled into the parking lot anyway. My five-year-old had wanted to see where I'd been baptized and where his grandparents had gotten married. As we sat and looked at the Masonic Lodge and Fredrik peppered me with questions for which I had no answers ("No idea where we used to park." "Not sure which door the bride and groom came out of." "I don't know if they served cookies afterward."), I got a little shiver. The sort that comes sometimes when I sense God coming especially close, close enough to feel the tingle and zap of holy presence.

And then I realized: Although I had no memory of ever attending this church, this was not only where my parents had married but where they had the good sense to take me as an infant to be christened, to be marked as one of God's own. This was the place where family friends became my beloved godparents and, after, huge influences in my life. This was the place where in all reality my wild-and-wooly, twisty-and-turny faith journey began. Though the Masons called it home, in all reality, this was *my* faith home.

Though I hadn't paid much mind to St. Luke's or the role it had in my life or my relationship with God, at least one pastor there—at one time—had. Years ago, as our wedding day approached, I called the church to get a copy of my baptismal record. Though we were getting married in my own (Christian Reformed) church, my husband and I wanted our marriage recognized by the Catholic church of his youth. So the first step in seeking a dispensation from the Archdiocese of Chicago was to prove my baptism.

I picked up the phone from my corner office, overlooking Chicago's Lyric Opera House, and called St. Luke's. The pastor answered the phone. I told him my predicament, and he was eager to help. While he flipped through files (or so I imagined), he asked questions. At first they were light: Where did I go to church now? Where had I gone to college? What line of work was I in? But then he deepened them: What had God done in my life since I left St. Luke's?

I laughed it off, "That's a big question to ask a busy bride-to-be!"

But, of course, I joked because I didn't want to answer. I didn't want to tell this strange, inquiring pastor that God hadn't been doing much—as far as I was concerned. I didn't want to tell him that, a few years before, I had sat on the side of a mountain and had asked for God to do *something*—for him to fill me with the Holy Spirit and let me *feel* God as I had when I was little—and had gotten nada.

At the time, I was years away from praying a similar prayer and was decades away from the unraveling of all things financial, from this time of learning, again, to stumble into God's presence and goodness mysteriously, serendipitously, cross-ily, shockingly, in each other, and so on. But being the people-pleaser I am, when the pastor asked again by saying, "He must be up to something since you're getting married in a church," I gave in. I muttered some stuff about becoming a Christian at seven but always having lots of questions—ones that sometimes got me in trouble for asking, but ones that strangely made me want to know more about God, and even love him more. He laughed, told me he'd found my record and asked where to send it. Then he wrapped up our conversation by asking if he could offer me a blessing over the phone.

"Sure," I said. "It'd be nice."

"May God walk with you and your husband on your marriage journey," he said. "And may you see with you God on every road life takes you, in the sunny spots as well as the cloudy ones."

I thanked the pastor and then jotted down his words, to show my fiancé later. But I gave them little thought at the time. My mind was, after all, on my wedding and my marriage. Not on spotting God. Not on considering any cloudy spots that might lie ahead. But when I dug the note out of the box that holds our wedding notes, receipts, well-wishes and whatnot—from between the pages of notes from my church's premarital counseling sessions and Rafi's church's "pre-Cana"[1] marriage-preparation weekend—the beauty and power of this blessing hit me. What this man—who didn't know me, who didn't even baptize me, but who, nevertheless, recognized his role in my faith life—asked for from God "came true."

Or, in reality, came back. Because, once upon a time, I'd been a champion at spotting God. At some point in the journey (growing up, I suppose) I lost the gift. Now, just as I strain to see the woodpeckers my kids point out, I'd stopped seeing God, lurking, shining, sitting, walking—whatever he's doing—in my midst.

But I'd also stopped looking. As my life took me through financial riches and then into financial poverty, as I walked through excess and then debt, and later as we went from no employment and a bleak future to jobs and books and sun-rising, I realized God had been there at every step, at every stop.

My friend Tracey takes issue with people saying, "God showed up." Rightfully so. If we believe in God—*the* God—we don't believe he comes and goes. He's around. All the time. He's present and at work. All the time. He's good and he loves us. All the time. And he sees and he hears us. All the time. All along our journeys.

Erasmus said it this way: "Bidden or not bidden, God is present."[2] Carl Jung hung these words above his door. I kind of want to too. It's too important to forget. Too true to succumb to our doubts. Whether or not we invite him, God is with us. Can't shake the Guy, really.

One of my most prized possessions is a watercolor painting of a rhino. It is painted by Betsey Fowler, who is married to Jim Fowler, the host of *Mutual of Omaha's Wild Kingdom*. From what I understand, while her husband was on location, Betsey would accompany him and sketch wildlife, which she would later paint.

What makes my painting particularly wonderful is that below it, on the matte, are words in gold scrawl, supposedly straight from Jim's journal the day Betsey sketched the rhino: "Fowler Expedition—filming diary—Large male rino [sic] at watering hole in Samburu, Kenya. These Rino [sic] are very powerful and you must be careful around them. I'm filming—Betsey sketching."

My mother saw this painting years ago at a special exhibition at the luxury retailer Neiman-Marcus, of all places. She fell in love with the scribbles and the colors and the rhino and the little bird on his back, and she knew it would make a perfect gift for me. Mom was right.

My animal-loving nature has long meant that an African safari is my all-time dream vacation. In fact, when I was in college, I almost fell in love with a man as he told me of his family's recent trip to Kenya. The safari he described was the sort rich people take: days spent bumping along in Land Rovers, pointing out zebras and wildebeests and giraffes, hoping to spot a lion. Nights were spent in lush tents, under mosquito nets, drinking imported wine, eating local food and listening to local legends. It sounded (and still sounds) perfect.

So not only do I love this watercolor—a study in pencil sketches with greens and blues and a half-an-orange sun—I love what it represents. Besides the love and thoughtfulness of my mother, of course, the painting somehow captures all of what a safari would mean to me—or, at least, the scribble on the bottom does. I love that the Fowlers shared an "expedition" and that, though they were together, each discovered a different something wonderful on their journey. And while I have zero desire to sit close enough to a rhino to sketch it (I don't draw), I do long to sit close enough to smell it, maybe, and to write about it, certainly (though no one could do this better than Rick Bass in *The Black Rhinos of Namibia*). Because there's just no way you can do that and have your life not be changed, not be affected.

That's the thing about safaris, right? You don't just go to see wildlife; you go to change your life.

But when my mother gave me this painting a year or so into my marriage, when we were busy saving for a down payment and I was realizing that magazine editing was never going to make me rich enough for my dream safari (even if my husband's business held promise), I figured the painting was as close to safari as I'd ever get. In fact, I hadn't thought about going on safari for years. Until my daughter brought home a worksheet from her second-grade unit on South Africa, that is.

Safari, according to her worksheet, is Swahili for "long journey." It comes from the Arabic word *safra* for the same. As I walked that worksheet from the backpack to the recycle bin, I realized, I may not ever get that rich-person's Kenyan dream safari, but I don't need to. I've been on one all along.

In Cheryl Strayed's bestselling book *Wild,* she recounts her 1,100-mile trek across the grueling and beautiful Pacific Crest Trail, a trek she undertook mostly because she was beaten down by hardship and heartbreak and was headed down a dangerous path in life. Knowing she needed change—something to jar her out of her figuratively dangerous path—Strayed chose a literal one. A path she hoped would help her "find herself," heal her wounds and set her straight. So, although she'd never hiked anywhere before, and though she had no clue what she was in for, Strayed headed out, alone, on a journey through the wilderness.

It's a wonderful story, a book good enough for Oprah to consider relaunching her book club, in fact. Strayed is a master writer; her prose dazzles and delights even when describing the harrowing. In fact, while reading this, I often marveled at how much Strayed's writing reminded me of David's psalms—the beauty of the language, the rugged and desperateness of the environment, and the stunning displays of God's creation and his intervention.

Of course, there's one (or probably a few) big difference: David recognizes God's hand as he wanders through the wilderness. Yet, straight through to the end, Strayed never does. For the Jesus-y set, this means that even as the book ends on a high note (speaking figuratively only; it ends with a literal descent) with Strayed's "healing," with her being found, we can't shake a sadness for all Strayed missed on her journey. Because *we* see God there with her, in the beauty, in her stamina, in the warning rattle of a snake's tail, in the goodness of the people she met, in the protection from the few "bad" ones. We see God reaching out to her. But Strayed never does.[3]

Of course, even those of us who believe in God, who profess that he is with us always, have a hard time seeing God on our own journeys too. And yet, in many ways, it's in the present moments, in the twists and turns, in the harrowing and sketchy, in the rough climbs and emotional descents that God is most evident. If we're willing to take note.

After finding my old Brownie "I Spy Hike" award in a tangle of childhood memorabilia, my daughter wanted to know my secrets so she could become an I Spy champ herself. I told her that to win at I Spy is to realize that I Spy is really a misnomer—because when we speak of "spying" something, we really mean "seeing" it. In fact, whether you're an international spy or simply a bird-and-squirrel spy, spying requires much more than eyesight. So when my kids and I are wandering through woods or along creek beds—hoping to spy a deer, chipmunk or one of those badgery-woodchuck-prairie dog guys—I tell them to be quiet, to step lightly, to breathe gently and to almost become *one* with the path we're on. That way, while we don't scare off animals who are as eager to run from us as we are to see them, we also become in tune with the world around us and are able to hear, feel, see or smell the animals we seek.

Of course, my kids think I'm out of my mind. But they aren't I Spy champs like me.

So when they roll their eyes as I become hyperaware on our walks, they miss that our journey is more than just a walk in a patch of suburban woods, more than a trek through a trail that borders the Sanitation Department. Instead we are transcending, and the journey transcends. So it is with us and God on this journey through life. We can plod along on our journey, heads down—busy with the present things, worried about the future things, regretful of the past things—or we can skip along the journey, smiles bright—cheering the present, hopeful for the future, shrugging off the past. But if we aren't mindful, if we aren't aware, if we aren't noticing, if we aren't "one" with our surroundings, then we miss so much. Most of all, we miss Who is next to us on that safari, Who has gone ahead of us on it, and Who is behind us, sweeping away our missteps and mistakes and redeeming them for what comes next.

As I type, there's a God meme getting some good play on Facebook. Were I to click over, I'd guess it'd show up in my newsfeed from seven different friends. It's a black-and-white, silly cartoon takeoff of the old "Footprints in the Sand" picture. In one panel of this cartoon, we see Jesus (or a God-looking guy,

I'm not sure) and a man at the beach. Jesus has his arm around the man and is saying, "My child, I never left you. Those places with one set of footprints? It was then that I carried you." In the next panel, Jesus points and says, "That long groove over there is when I dragged you for a while."[4]

While I'm not sure the theology of this cartoon lines up with my understanding of free will, the point is well taken—at least, it is if the point is that we need to pay attention to where we are and where God is in our walks along life's beaches, up life's mountains, over life's deserts, or even life's rockets right over the moon. That God is "God with us" in each and every one of the places we trek through in life should never slip our minds. And sometimes, when we are so weary, so unable to take another step, God does sweep in and carry us, maybe even drag us a bit if we've given ourselves to him and his leading, if we've asked him to take us where we should be. We should not only turn around every now and again to see where he *has* been with us, but we should look to see where he is now and where he'll be tomorrow and the next day.

Because if God is anything, he's a God who journeys with his people, who hitches right along in the Land Rover on our safaris through life. He's there bumping along, pointing out zebras, spotting the lions, then tucking us in below the mosquito netting with a good meal and story of his legendary love.

The Old Testament is not exactly filled with or known for its "precious moments." But when one of those moments appears, it's hard not to sigh and bring a hand to your heart, thinking of how mighty and just plain sweet our God is. This is what happened to me smack dab in the middle of the not-so-soft-and-cuddly 1 Kings. But in the eighteenth and nineteenth chapters, we find the prophet Elijah in a mess of trouble. Jezebel wants him dead and he hits the road. After dropping his servant off in Beersheba, Elijah takes off for the wilderness alone. Just one day in, the fear, the hunger, the exhaustion has caught hold of him. Elijah has had enough, and he crawls under a "broom bush" and prays "that he might die."

God apparently has a soft spot for people crawling under bushes to die (and I have a soft spot for the stories of God's soft spot), because after letting Elijah sleep a bit, an angel swings by, touches Elijah on the shoulder, and tells him to get up and eat. Elijah looks over and sees fresh-baked bread and a jar of water. He eats it and falls back asleep.

The angel comes back, and this time, says the loveliest thing: "Get up and eat, for the journey is too much for you." I'm no angel expert, but it seems to me that since other times in Scripture angels appear as *messengers* from God—with their "do not fears" and "glad tidings"—it isn't too much of a stretch to see this as a sign of our mighty God's empathy for his children. This is God at his most maternal, offering food and drink and a comforting hand on a sleepy child, saying, "There, there . . ."

After resting, Elijah heads up to Horeb, "the mountain of God," where God reveals himself once again in one of the most amazing scenes in Scripture.

> And the word of the LORD came to him: "What are you doing here, Elijah?"
>
> He replied, "I have been very zealous for the LORD God Almighty. The Israelites have rejected your covenant, torn down your altars, and put your prophets to death with the sword. I am the only one left, and now they are trying to kill me too."

The LORD said, "Go out and stand on the mountain in the presence of the LORD, for the LORD is about to pass by."

Then a great and powerful wind tore the mountains apart and shattered the rocks before the LORD, but the LORD was not in the wind. After the wind there was an earthquake, but the LORD was not in the earthquake. After the earthquake came a fire, but the LORD was not in the fire. And after the fire came a gentle whisper. When Elijah heard it, he pulled his cloak over his face and went out and stood at the mouth of the cave. (1 Kings 19:9-13)

I love this because Elijah *recognized* the Lord. Elijah recognized the angel, recognized God's speaking voice and recognized the Lord in a whisper after quite the creation show. I love that Elijah understood that, although God is capable of whipping up and being in avalanche-starting windstorms, of shaking the very earth on which he stood and of sparking flames, the Lord was not in those. I love that Elijah knew God enough—was in tune with him enough—to recognize God in the comparatively silent.

It's an astonishing skill, really. But not one only for Old Testament prophets. I believe it's available to all of us, and we learn it—the ability to recognize God and his revelations—through our journeys.

"What do you think is the best way to 'grow your soul'?" Laura asked.

A room full of us groaned. A few of us piped up.

"Suffering."

"Heartache."

"Pain."

"Navigating the horrible twists and turns of life."

And then a room full of us laughed. It's not the sort of stuff Christians put in our evangelistic tracts, but really, it's true: if we want to grow our souls, to develop spiritually, to mature in the faith, the only way to do that is by traversing some rough road of life. I wish it could happen more easily. I wish that when I prayed that God would "increase my faith" he could've done it by lavishing on me nonstop happiness and riches and bestselling books to "prove" how faithful he is. Instead, I got stress, near-bankruptcy and, well, let's just say: thank *you* for reading this book.

But it's on the journey through life—even the rough parts, the parts that make us, like Elijah, want to crawl under broom bushes and beg for God to take us—that we ultimately learn to taste and see, to hear and know, to feel and smell that God is with us. That every last step we take is indeed taken in God's presence, is indeed taken on holy ground. Every step! Every step!

It can be so hard to realize, so hard to learn, but it's so worth doing.

This summer, one hour into our return trip from that glorious week at my friend's cabin—the one in which I'd felt God dazzle and delight me, about which my son Henrik declared the "best trip ever"—our car broke down. Me, my husband, three kids, one dog and a trunk full of luggage, stranded in the middle of the Northwoods, six miles from the nearest town, on a Sunday afternoon.

My first instinct was to once again raise a fist at God and then start crying, "Why, oh why, oh why?!?!" My second instinct was to immediately panic about money, wondering if we could cover the cost of a hotel *and* a God-knows-what repair. But when I turned around to settle my kids, I realized I had to ignore those instincts and perhaps walk my talk a bit.

So I faked my best cool-and-collected mom voice and said,

"This stinks. But you know what? It's an opportunity for God to show us how he can take care of us."

My oldest (the one most like me) immediately rolled his eyes and started with "If he took care of us, why are we on the side of the road?"

I conceded his point and offered an "I don't know why we're here, but I do know he's going to help us."

While my husband talked to the roadside-assistance dispatcher, he shook his head at my fake chipperness. I might not have been convincing my family of my newfound uber-faithfulness, but I was going to keep trying. And I think God must've noticed my good effort. Because, after being rescued by the tow-truck driver and the owner of the garage who drove out separately to give my family (and dog) a ride into town, we found refuge at the local Holiday Inn Express, where we found dog-friendly hospitality, a pool, free breakfast, and entertainment in the form of being within walking distance to a Walmart, a Goodwill *and* a Culver's.

As we changed into our bathing suits for a dip in the pool and a soak in the hot tub, I asked my kids to tell me if they'd experienced God at work at all in our rescue.

My daughter said God knew that, as much as she loved the cabin, she really loves vacations with *pools*, so he gave her one.

My youngest son said he always wanted to ride in a pickup truck and now he'd gotten to.

My oldest just rolled his eyes at me again. As did my husband.

I offered what I had seen. I knew God was helping us, I told them, because when we checked in, the woman at the front desk crossed off a portion of our dog agreement. Because the woman had already petted our sweet Sierra in the lobby and clearly had recognized her pit-bull-ness. So, as she ran her Sharpie through the dog-discriminatory language prohibiting pit-bull-types and

Rottweilers and smiled at me, I felt that whispery-wind that Elijah recognized. Had I been wearing a cloak or in a mountain cave, I might have pulled it up and stepped outside to feel the Lord pass by.

God revealed himself through rescue, through shelter and then through the kindness of strangers. I still can't tell my kids (or my husband or myself) why God allowed the car to break down or if he even had much to do with it at all. But I know that God was with us on our journey, every step, every rotation of the tires, and I knew that God would be with us still as we got our car back the next day—as we paid the bill for the forty-dollar (!) fix, as we traveled down through the woods and into the farms and then the college towns and then the cities and the suburbs and then home.

God was with us. The whole road, the whole way, our whole life, with me, my husband and my family, at every twist, at every turn—from the moment my husband and I checked into our honeymoon suite and heard the bizarre words of our would-be-prophet bellhop to the moment I understood the truth of them, God was there. As we ventured into life, greeted by mountain-high successes and valley-low failures and every boring, learn-nothing plateau in between, God was there.

As I lived the prophet-bellhop's words—where my family had lost so much (financially) but gained immeasurably more (spir-itually, eternally, whatever-ly)—God was there and so, so good.

Right at the end of the glorious Twenty-Third Psalm, David writes, "Surely your goodness and love will follow me all the days of my life."

How I love that image. God's goodness, his love, his self, tagging along as we trek through life. As we angry-stomp through woods, as we walk down hospital corridors, as we pass by kids' new schools. As we slip into church, as we sink onto sofas, collapsing in shame and hurt and brokenness, God's goodness and mercy follow us every step of our journeys, on every path of our safaris.

We just need to turn around. And notice. And then and there, we will always find God and find him good.

Appendix

Ways to Practice Finding God's Abundance

⟩

I saw his hand first, then his head and then his squinty eyes ducked around the wall into our youngest son's room.

"You seen my glasses?" my husband whispered.

I smiled and told our son I'd be right back to finish the tucking in.

I hate to call it the *worst* feeling in the world, but it comes close: not being able to find your glasses after you've already taken your contacts out. Looking for the thing you need to be able to see without actually being able to see is not fun.

While my husband *had* tried feeling around the bathroom a bit—opening drawers and reaching to feel if the glasses fell behind something—his other senses were of little value to him here. Rafi couldn't have sniffed out his glasses; he couldn't probably taste them even if he *had* wanted to lick the bathroom floor. And he really didn't *want* to hear them. That had happened to me not long before—that horrible back step and then crunch—an expensive misstep no one wants to repeat.

So, after squinting his way around the bathroom, doing his best search—if limited—Rafi did the reasonable thing: he asked for help.

I adjusted my own glasses and came into the bathroom like Super Vision Girl to the rescue. Immediately I saw what Rafi could not: the black "wing" (technically "temple") of the glasses sticking out from the black Dopp kit that hung next to the sink. Then, suddenly, Rafi could see; I went back to resume bedtime rituals and all was right with the world.

Sometimes we just need a little help, a little human intervention when it comes to being able to see God's wings poking out of Dopp kits too. So in the pages that follow, I'm getting explicit and practical with some ways that others have helped me see, hear, taste, touch, smell, and find God and his goodness in this world and in our lives.

Nothing here is rocket science or new. Rather, just consider these as practical tools—spiritual *disciplines* or *practices*—that give a hand in experiencing God when all else seems to be failing.

PRAYER

Obviously—or perhaps maybe not—if we want to experience God's presence, we need to recognize that God is real and acknowledge that God is communicable. Thus we should communicate with our very real God if we want to find God and find him good. In the Christian tradition, communicating with or talking to God is known as prayer. If you want to experience God, feel him, hear him, taste him, see him and so forth, you've got to pray to him.

Prayer takes many forms. You can free-form it, which I often do. You can use prayer books, which I sometimes do. You can use your body to help you: folding hands, kneeling, shaking fists, lifting arms, clenching and then opening fists, lying prostrate on the floor. I've been known to do any and all of these. You don't even need words: you can think prayer or squeal or grunt it. God is infinite-lingual. He speaks body language and Squeal and Grunt. Thank God.

But following are a few prayers I've found particularly wonderful during my seasons of feeling like God was not as near as I'd like.

The Lord's Prayer. I've written about the times in my life when I had no words to pray—when I could barely believe in God, let alone *talk* to him. These were the times when I'd either groan or grunt or cry, *or* I'd pray the words a zillion others had prayed before me, starting with the ones that Jesus taught us.

I've been praying a Lord's Prayer combo for years now. I pray it whether I'm in the mood to or not, whether I'm feeling particularly Jesus-y or connected to God or not. And I pray it like this:

Our Father
Who art in heaven
Hallowed be thy name.
Thy kingdom come;
Thy will be done
On earth as it is in heaven.
Give us this day our daily bread.
Forgive us our trespasses
As we forgive those who trespass against us.
Lead us not into temptation
But deliver us from evil.
For thine is the kingdom,
And the power and the glory
Forever.[1]

My Father
Who art in heaven
Hallowed be thy name.
Thy kingdom come;
Thy will be done
On earth as it is in heaven.
Give me (my family) this day my daily bread.

Forgive me my trespasses
As I forgive those who trespass against me.
Lead me not into temptation
But deliver me from evil.
For thine is the kingdom,
And the power and the glory
Forever.

Our Father
Who art in heaven
Hallowed be thy name.
Thy kingdom come;
Thy will be done
On earth as it is in heaven.
Give us this day our daily bread.
Forgive us our trespasses
As we forgive those who trespass against us.
Lead us not into temptation
But deliver us from evil.
For thine is the kingdom,
And the power and the glory
Forever.

Amen.

Much has been written about the importance of the community element of the Lord's Prayer, and I get that. I believe that! However, I sandwich in a little first-person version because it helps me remember that God doesn't only see me as part of a big mass of followers. Rather, he sees me as someone worth delivering daily bread to and as someone worth leading away from temptation and as someone worth extending plenty of grace and forgiveness.

I've often described this repeated time of morning prayer to be "centering." It's a word borrowed from the Buddhists, of course, but by it, I mean that it helps me understand my place in relation to this world and to God—and conversely, God's place in relation to this world and to me.

The Jesus Prayer. While I do not say this prayer as "religiously" as I might, the Jesus Prayer—a staple of Eastern Orthodox churches and first recorded by Diadochos of Photiki—is my go-to prayer when stress rises and I feel God moving beyond my grasp, when I imagine God shrinking backward into a light I can only squint at.

> Jesus, Son of God,
> have mercy on me,
> a sinner.

The image I imagine is not a correct one, of course—it's a lie born out of my fears and worries—so the Jesus Prayer helps me remember who Jesus is and what he offers. I tend to repeat this prayer until I get dry in the mouth or until a better image of God, one of him walking with me—even if it is through floods and flames—returns.

The Worrywart Prayer. In her book *Everything,* Mary DeMuth offers this prayer. I don't mean to be overly dramatic, but this prayer changed my life—or, at least, my perspective. I loved the specificity of it and the imagery. Perfect for the times when *worry* gets in the way of me noticing God.

So I typed it up, printed it out and tacked it above my desk. While I'm usually quite selective in my routine prayers (as I only use two others, and they have impressive pedigree and longevity!), DeMuth's "Worrywart Prayer" had me at, well, *worrywart*:

> Dear Jesus, I give You _____. I
> humble myself before You, believing that You are bigger

than I am, that You are more capable to handle my burdens. I don't know what the outcome of my giving up control of _____ will be, but even so, I open my fist and let You grab it (or the person) from me. I want Your will. I want Your presence. I need Your strength. Please take this burden today, and use it in my life for Your glory. Help me to entrust _____ to You even when things seem dark. I trust You. At least, I try. But help me trust You today. I give it up. I choose not to worry anymore about this. Amen.[2]

Prayers of thanksgiving. Gratitude lists have been getting a lot of press these days, particularly thanks to the recent runaway, bestselling success of Ann Voskamp's *One Thousand Gifts*—a book about living a grateful life.

For much of my life, I'd found gratitude lists to be annoying as all get out. I questioned people who spent time writing down words and phrases—like "daisies" or "shrimp toast" or "that great parking space"—as an act of any spiritual importance or depth. But that was *before* I ended up feeling bitter, ungrateful and like God was giving me zip, when in fact he was blessing me plenty.

And I credit my youngest son with turning my attitude around. While he is a great kid and fun and funny, my boy likes stuff. He is—in a word—greedy. He asks for every toy we see and, when I *do* bribe him with a little something if he sits quietly in the conference-room corner and watches his movie nicely while Mama's in yet another meeting, he'll grumble and complain if the bribe-toy turns out to be less "big" than he imagined.

Let's just say: there's nothing like me giving a child a gift and being told it's not good enough to help me understand the importance of being grateful. Even for daisies and shrimp toast and great parking spaces. And I tell you: there's nothing that *can* turn a complaining heart around faster than listing all the things God has blessed me with. So now I keep lists. In an actual, official gratitude journal. I probably have well over a thousand things— as I've filled it with the inane and the amazing, the insignificant and the life-altering—but I cannot add to the list or read through past ones without recognizing God's amazing presence and goodness in my life.

Prayers of lament. Lament doesn't have nearly the level of popularity gratitude does. But it should. Lament is overlooked, undervalued and totally misunderstood. Far from being a sign of faithlessness or ingratitude, or even being the same as whining, lament plays a powerful role in the Christian life. Scripture is chock-full of lamenters. From Leah and Naomi, to David and the psalmists, to the prophets straight on through to Jesus, we read of faithful people who poured out their hearts and griev-ances to God. And we read of a God who not only accepted their laments but seemed to bless them.

Laments "work" in helping us experience God's nearness be-cause it's through lament that we are able to bring our honest, open hearts to God—at least, when we're grieving. We know that the Christian life is not always smiles and sunshine but often thunderclouds and tears, so it's essential that we have lan-guage to use to come before God *both* in praise and thanksgiving *and* in lament.

That said, we don't want to become constant complainers, so I believe it's essential that we establish "criteria" for our griev-ances—so we don't end up actually whining about every last thing. For me, I know when I need to grieve or cry out to God if something (1) breaks my heart, (2) is lost or (3) is something I cannot change.[3]

What also keeps a lament from becoming an all-out whine or

a self-centered gripe is the matter of where it ends up. While I believe in bringing God all the down-and-dirty details of whatever is wrong with my world (he knows it anyway!), a lament really works its "magic" in what I call the "and yet" moment. This is the place where, after you have laid it all bare before God, you acknowledge his goodness, his mercy, his grace, his very divinity. And it's in this moment where God swoops right on in.

For great examples of this, check out two of my favorite laments: Psalm 13 and Habakkuk 3:17-19.

Prayers of confession. Sin keeps us from fellowship with God. While Jesus' death on the cross and gift of grace creates that "bridge" between us and God, if we're in a spot where sin is ruling our lives and we are unrepentant, we need to confess and seek God's forgiveness. God *knows* our sins and freely offers forgiveness, so in many ways, it seems silly to go through the trouble of naming sins and asking for forgiveness. But in the same way that listing the things for which we are grateful and about which we mourn draws us closer to God, so does confessing our sins.

I know this from experience: an unrepentant heart has a hard time communing with our gracious God.

SPIRITUAL PRACTICES

Lectio divina. I first learned about the ancient practice of *lectio divina* years ago while editing a marriage workbook. Since that time, I've heard and seen it led, and have read about it being done lots of different ways. So many ways, in fact, I'm not even sure which is correct—or if there is a correct way.

All I know is that *lectio divina,* which means "holy reading," is a way of reading through Scripture that some have described as allowing "Scripture to read you." It sounds creepy and ooky-spooky (probably why I love it), but it's amazing. God speaks through *lectio divina*. Time and time again. It *is* his Word, after all.

Here is my preferred *lectio* method:

1. Find a quiet space—either alone or with a group of people.

2. Pick a passage of Scripture (following a lectionary can be helpful here).

3. Read through it.

4. Read through it again, asking God to highlight or impress a particular word or phrase on your heart or mind.

5. Read through it one last time, asking God to confirm that word or phrase.

6. Linger on that word or phrase, letting your soul steep in it a bit.

This soul-steeping part is what I think of as the "Maybe God Is Trying to Tell You Something" part, when as sung straight out of the fantastic reconciliation scene between Shug Avery and her pastor dad in *The Color Purple*, I believe God often tries to tell us things and that, often, we just aren't listening. Engaging in the practice of *lectio divina* means we've quieted ourselves and our souls enough to hear what God wants us to hear.

I should also say that while *lectio* can be done individually, I tend to space out, so when I do them alone, I need to do just a quick *lectio* or a "mini-*lectio*" as I call them. For this reason, though, I really love to do group *lectios*. I love the conversation that follows—especially when it seems that God has had similar things to say to many of us. And I love when we can share what, maybe, God *is* trying to tell us—and then to know that about one another. The beauty of hearing God speak through his Word straight into our hearts is that this also translates into the beauty of sharing God's words to us with others.

Examen. Though I credit my pal Tracey Bianchi for getting me hooked on the examen (one of the most powerful "tools" for recognizing God's presence and goodness throughout the day), Ignatius Loyola—father of the Jesuits—gets the real credit for it. According to Loyola Press's Ignatian Spirituality website, "One of the few rules of prayer that Ignatius made for the Jesuit order was the requirement that Jesuits practice the Examen twice daily—at noon and at the end of the day. It's a habit that Jesuits, and many other Christians, practice to this day."[4]

For good reason. Ignatius considered the practice a gift from God, and I'd like to agree with him.

The purpose of the examen is to begin by reflecting *back* on a day and seeing where God's hand was, perhaps, most at work. Once we get good at reflecting back and seeing this, it also helps us recognize God's hand in the present—and even discern where it might lead in the future.

When my friend Tracey first walked me through a very casual version of the examen, she asked questions like: *Where has God felt near in my day? Where has he felt far away?* And others have suggested: *Where have I been like Jesus? Where I have been quite un-Jesus-y?*

I do a super casual version of this with my kids each day when I ask, after school, "What was the most wonderful, excellent, gooey-chocolate-brownie part of the day?" and "What was the most horrible, icky, poke-sticks-in-your-eye part?"

But, of course, Ignatius had a more formal five-step version of the daily examen, which is a wonderful place to start:

1. Become aware of God's presence.

2. Review the day with gratitude.

3. Pay attention to your emotions.

4. Choose one feature of the day and pray from it.

5. Look toward tomorrow.[5]

Read the Scriptures. If we want to hear God, the easiest, no-nonsense way to do it is by going to his book, right? But I've found that the Bible not only gives us direct words from God, it also offers plenty of "clues" on how we can better experience God in our daily lives.

In nature. One of my favorite verses—and one my mother often paraphrased to me—is Luke 19:40. Jesus shouts over his disciples to tell the intent-on-silencing-the-crowd Pharisees: "If they keep quiet, the stones will cry out."

Hard to see a stone the same way again. But this also seemed to be a nice confirmation that the psalmist knew of what he wrote in Psalm 96:11-13:

> Let the heavens rejoice, let the earth be glad;
>   let the sea resound, and all that is in it.
> Let the fields be jubilant, and everything in them;
>   let all the trees of the forest sing for joy.
> Let all creation rejoice before the LORD, for he comes,
>   he comes to judge the earth.

So many more of the psalms offer us pictures of nature worshiping God that it becomes difficult to encounter any of the world without seeing God being worshiped—and present—in it. Psalm 98:2 tells us "The LORD has made his salvation known and revealed his righteousness to the nations." Later we read: "Let the sea resound, and everything in it, the world, and all who live in it. Let the rivers clap their hands, let the mountains sing together for joy" (vv. 7-8).

Read through the Psalms; let your eyes, ears, nose, tongue and hands be open to sensing God's presence in this world.

Cheat off the Prophets. One of the best ways to learn to see, hear, taste, smell and feel God everywhere is to, frankly, cheat: copy how other people do it! And by "other people," here I mean the biblical prophets. Clearly, the prophets had a connection and intimacy with God many of us do not. We're not gifted this way. But this is not to say we shouldn't we pay attention to the ways they've encountered God, especially when they delivered messages *from* God on how to commune with him.

Isaiah 55:6—part of the "Invitation to the Thirsty" passage—offers lovely cadence and an even lovelier truth: "Seek the LORD while he may be found; call on him while he is near." And when is God nearest? Isaiah 58:6-9 offers a clue:

> Is not this the kind of fasting I have chosen:
> to loose the chains of injustice
>   and untie the cords of the yoke,
> to set the oppressed free
>   and break every yoke?
> Is it not to share your food with the hungry
>   and to provide the poor wanderer with shelter—
> when you see the naked, to clothe them,
>   and not to turn away from your own flesh and blood?
> Then your light will break forth like the dawn,
>   and your healing will quickly appear;
> then your righteousness will go before you,
>   and the glory of the LORD will be your rear guard.
> Then you will call, and the LORD will answer;
>   you will cry for help, and he will say: Here am I.

Plenty of other passages offer clues as well. Psalm 34:18 tells us that God is close to the brokenhearted. James 4:7-10 says:

> Submit yourselves, then, to God. Resist the devil, and he will flee from you. Come near to God and he will come near to you. Wash your hands, you sinners, and purify your hearts, you double-minded. Grieve, mourn and wail.

Change your laughter to mourning and your joy to gloom.
Humble yourselves before the Lord, and he will lift you up.

But of course, every time we read the Word of God, we are near. We hear and feel God's breath, the story of his love in each sentence and page.

Corporate worship. While I'm quite Reformed in my thinking, and I believe that we can and do worship God in *all* we do, the truth is that if we want to feel and see and know and smell and taste and hear God, then heading to his house is a wise move. There's just nothing like—if you ask me—having a bunch of sinners coming off of a bunch of stressful weeks and Saturday nights, wrestling a bunch of demons and struggling with a bunch of weaknesses, all coming together to lift voices and hands and words and hearts and souls to God.

Trust and obey. When I was a child, we'd sing the old song "Trust and Obey." The premise was as the chorus says: we trust and obey "to be happy in Jesus." That's a nice enough idea, I suppose, but through much of my life that didn't cut it. Especially when I could be "happy" in so many other sinful things. Why obey?

Obedience isn't about making us happy, not necessarily at least. It's about—as it's been said a million times before—making us holy. But beyond that, when we obey, that very act of trust brings us into tight communion with God. The act of obedience sets us on a path of being able to see, hear, taste, smell, feel and know God in so many ways. The decision to obey serves, in many ways, as a benchmark for entering God's presence, for our particular bit of holy ground.

Because even when that ground feels unsure or we can't see the next step as clearly as we like, when we obey, when we trust, we learn to rely on and experience God with all we've got.

Confession. But here's another thing about trusting and obeying: we'll fail. God knows this. Jesus died for this. But still, in living a life where we don't trust and where we don't obey, we have a harder time sensing God's goodness and living his goodness.

So when we fail to trust, when we fail to obey, when we stumble on purpose or on accident, we need to confess. It's an icky process—or can be. Some "stumbles" are easy to apologize for, but others are tougher—particularly the ones we don't want to admit to being stumbles because, maybe, we stumbled over something we're pretty sure we deserved or because we're pretty sure that person had it coming.

My pastor has used a wheelbarrow image to describe sin—or the effects of it. We all have wheelbarrows that we're carrying around with us through life, filled with different "sin" bricks. It's through repentance and accepting grace that we empty our wheelbarrows and "lighten our loads." I didn't start out liking this image much. Like so many Christian images, I fought it.

Though my pastor doesn't use it to highlight any one type of sin above others, plenty do. So it's easy to acknowledge the fornication or adulterous bricks, the drunken bricks, the addiction bricks, the murder bricks, the armed-robbery bricks, the debt bricks. It's not a stretch to imagine how they weigh down our lives, keeping us from finding God.

However, I got a better image of *my* wheelbarrow when I stopped fighting the image. While certainly many of those "big"-sin bricks have weighed down my wheelbarrow from time to time, when I sat for a moment with this picture, I didn't see a brick-weighted wheelbarrow but a mud-splattered, muck-covered one. Though I'd confessed—and gotten rid of—the big sins, I'd failed to scrape off and shake out the remnant sins, the "smaller" but stickier stuff. And, in truth, it was this muck and mud that weighed my wheelbarrow down. That was what was getting in the way of me and God. And I needed to lose it.

This is where confession, repentance and grace come in. There's no sweeter moment of God's presence and goodness than when we stop and recognize where we have "gone astray" (Isaiah 53:6)—where our hearts have wandered and where we have sinned—and when we remember the gift of grace Jesus offers and let him scrub our wheelbarrows clean.

Giving. I'd be remiss if—at the tail end of a book about how I found God and found him good amid financial calamity—I didn't talk about giving. This is the area where so many criticize the church—like all churches want is people's money. And while, perhaps, this *is* what some churches or preachers or organizations are after, it's not what God's about.

He doesn't need our money and he doesn't want our cash. God wants us to trust him with our financial resources and love him more than our money. When we give (aside from helping others, which of course is a huge component of this), and give faithfully and generously, we show this love and trust.

Of course, through my own financial journey, I have failed at this discipline more than any other. Perhaps it's because *giving* is my "top" spiritual gift that I've failed so dramatically. But it's been hard, when faced with losing so much, to keep giving. God and I (and my husband) are still working through this.

But I want to give—long to give—because I know that, when we offer up what we barely have, and when we hand over what we so desperately need, we find God and we find him good.

Acknowledgments

So much gratitude. So little space . . .

Thanks to all the folks who have stood with me while writing this book—not only with the writing, but with the circumstances surrounding it. Thanks to the friends and family who have supported me—us—in so many ways.

Thanks to the amazing women in my writers group for your feedback and encouragement. Thanks to my pastors, Rev. Peter Semeyn and Rev. Gregg DeMey, for answering questions and just generally putting up with me and my odd streak of Reformed mysticism. And also, thanks for hiring me.

Thanks to my agent, Andrea Heinecke, for shopping this around and handling the nitty-gritty that I hate so much. Thanks to the fine folks at IVP: Cindy Bunch for sticking with the most disastrous first draft I've ever turned in, for seeing the real story poking through the gnarled chapters and for helping me grab hold of it; to Elaina Whittenhall for her marvelous edits; to Allison Rieck for her proofreading mastery and to Cindy Kiple for her wonderful cover design. Thanks also to Lorraine Caulton, Krista Carnet, Alisse Wissman and Adrianna Wright for championing this project.

Thanks to my kids, Henrik, Greta and Fredrik. It's not easy to have a mom who writes about embarrassing stuff like debt and talking to Jesus on the back porch. (Sorry!) And thanks to my husband, Rafi. Ditto about the not easy. Thanks for being a believer in vulnerability and openness and who-cares-what-they-thinkness. You're the best.

And to God: gee, thanks. No really, thanks. Thanks for breaking me clean and wide open. Thanks for letting all the gook and junk run free. And thanks for standing by to help mop it up and glue me back together, better than ever. Thanks for blessing me by breaking me. And thank you, thank you, thank you for letting me figure this out by writing it down. And with a book deal where I could make a few (few) bucks in the process. You're smirking again, aren't you?

Notes

CHAPTER 2: BREAD

[1]Laura Story, "Blessings," *Blessings* (Franklin, TN: Brentwood-Benson Music, 2011).

[2]Jonathan Martin, "Gender, Race, and Pentecost: The World Has Moved On," July 24, 2012, http://pastorjonathanmartin.com/uncategorized/gender-race-and-pentecost-the-world-has-moved-on.

CHAPTER 3: MYSTERIES

[1]Chopin, "The Funeral March," *Piano Sonata No. 2 in B-flat minor, Op. 35.*

[2]Of course, this was in 1979–1980. The church wouldn't have officially "taught" this anymore. But, you know, Vatican II rolled out a little slow in some areas.

CHAPTER 4: BIG FISH

[1]I'm forever grateful to my astute sister-in-law Gina for picking up on this in *Grumble Hallelujah!*

CHAPTER 5: CROSSES

[1]Sarah Styles Bessey, "Incarnation," *A Deeper Story* blog, December 14, 2011, http://deeperstory.com/incarnation/.

[2]Of course, I cannot write this without thinking of women who long to bear children but either cannot or have not. These words will hurt to read. As someone who has gone through infertility, I know. I get the ache, the longing, the desire, and I understand how reading this will add salt to fresh wounds. I need to say that these unfulfilled longings for children, or even childbirth, also connect women to God, to sacrifice and to the

cross in ways that women who have given birth cannot understand. Certainly, childbirth is but one example of how God is reflected in women—and not the only, or even the best, one.

CHAPTER 7: SHOCKED

[1] Kate Atkinson, *When Will There Be Good News?* (New York: Little, Brown and Company, 2008), p. 352.
[2] Henri J. M. Nouwen, *Eternal Seasons: A Spiritual Journey Through the Church's Year,* ed. Michael Ford, rev. ed. (Notre Dame, IN: Ave Maria Press, 2007), p. 38.

CHAPTER 8: SERENDIPITY

[1] Abraham Verghese, *Cutting for Stone* (New York: Vintage Books, 2009), p. 648.
[2] Morton A. Meyers, *Happy Accidents: Serendipity in Modern Medical Breakthroughs* (New York: Arcade Publishing, 2007).
[3] Jill Neimark, "The Power of Coincidence," *Psychology Today,* July 1, 2004, www.psychologytoday.com/articles/200407/the-power-coincidence.

CHAPTER 9: IMAGINARY

[1] They are Clio, Thalia, Erato, Euterpe, Polyhymnia, Calliope, Terpsichore, Urania and Melpomene.
[2] Jonalyn Fincher, "How to Have Conversations with God," blog post on the Positively Human website, April 16, 2012, http://soulation.org/positivelyhuman/?p=842.
[3] Frank C. Laubach, *Letters by a Modern Mystic* (Colorado Springs: Purposeful Design Publications, 2007) p. 41.
[4] Tanya Luhrmann, "Why Women Hear God More Than Men Do," *Christianity Today,* May 7, 2012, www.christianitytoday.com/ct/2012/mayweb-only/why-women-hear-god.html.

CHAPTER 10: DAZZLED

[1] Anne Lamott announced this on her Facebook page on July 26, 2012, referring to *Help, Thanks, Wow: The Three Essential Prayers* (New York: Riverhead, 2012).
[2] Sarah Pulliam Bailey, "Pod People: Treat Religion News Like Crime

News," *Patheos*, July 28, 2012, www.patheos.com/blogs/getreligion/2012/07/why-cant-we-treat-religion-reporting-like-crime-reporting.

[3]Albert Haase, *Living the Lord's Prayer: The Way of the Disciple* (Downers Grove, IL: IVP Books, 2009), p. 53.

[4]Quoted by Keith Simon, "Christianity and Culture" blog post, Every Square Inch, February 23, 2012, www.everysquareinch.net/2012/02/christianity-and-culture.html.

CHAPTER 11: SAFARIS

[1]Catholic pre-Cana was a requirement for dispensation—not because we needed so much extra counseling!

[2]Quoted in Adele Ahlberg Calhoun, *Spiritual Disciplines Handbook* (Downers Grove, IL: InterVarsity Press, 2005), p. 30.

[3]Some of this wording first appeared in my "Book Review: Wild," *Today's Christian Woman*, November/December 2012, www.todayschristianwoman.com/articles/2012/novemberdecember-issue/book-review-wild.html. Used with permission.

[4]To see the cartoon, go to http://chainsawsuit.com/2012/08/08/footprints-in-the-sand-part-1/ from August 8, 2012.

APPENDIX: WAYS TO PRACTICE FINDING GOD'S ABUNDANCE

[1]Adapted from the Lutheran's Small Catechism.

[2]Mary DeMuth, *Everything: What You Give and What You Gain to Become Like Jesus* (Nashville: Thomas Nelson, 2012), p. 49.

[3]For more on this, see my book *Grumble Hallelujah* (Wheaton, IL: Tyndale Momentum, 2011).

[4]"The Daily Examen," IgnatianSpirituality.com, www.ignatianspirituality.com/ignatian-prayer/the-examen/.

[5]Ibid.

About the Author

Caryn Rivadeneira is a writer and speaker and serves on the worship ministry staff at Elmhurst Christian Reformed Church. She's the author of four other books: *Shades of Mercy* (River North, 2013), *Known and Loved: 52 Devotions from the Psalms* (Revell, 2013), *Grumble Hallelujah: Learning to Love Life When It Lets You Down* (Tyndale, 2011) and *Mama's Got a Fake I.D.: How to Reveal the Real You Behind All that Mom* (Waterbrook, 2009). Caryn is also a regular contributor to Christianity Today's *Hermeneutics*, Re:Frame Media's *Think Christian* and the Soulation blog. Her work regularly appears in several other media outlets, and you can hear Caryn regularly on Moody Radio's *Midday Connection*.

Caryn lives outside of Chicago with her husband, three kids and one pit bull.

For more information on having Caryn speak at your event, write for your publication or to share your own "broke" story:

Email Caryn at caryn@carynrivadeneira.com
Visit carynrivadeneira.com
Friend her on Facebook (Caryn Dahlstrand Rivadeneira)
Follow her on Twitter @CarynRivadeneir

A single-session book group
discussion guide for *Broke*
is available at ivpress.com.

www.ivpress.com/broke

A six-session discussion guide
is available at the author's website:
carynrivadeneira.com.

IVP *Crescendo*
COURAGE. CONFIDENCE. CALLING.

Some voices challenge us. Others support or encourage us. Voices can move us to change our minds, draw close to God, discover a new spiritual gift. The voices of others are shaping who we are.

The voices behind IVP Crescendo join together to draw us into God's story. We'll discover God's work around the globe even as we learn to love the people around the corner. We'll have opportunity to heal our places of pain. We'll discover new ways to love our families. We'll hear God's voice speaking into our lives as we discover new places of influence.

IVP Crescendo invites you to join in the rising chorus

- *to listen to the voices of others*
- *to hear the voice of God*
- *and to grow your own voice in*

COURAGE. CONFIDENCE. CALLING.

ivpress.com/crescendo
ivpress.com/crescendo-social